Ancient Egypt

Discovering Lost Stories from Egyptian History

Free Bonus from Captivating History
(Available for a Limited time)

Hi History Lovers!

Now you have a chance to join our exclusive history list so you can get your first history ebook for free as well as discounts and a potential to get more history books for free!

Simply visit the link below to join.

Or, Scan the QR code!

captivatinghistory.com/ebook

Also, make sure to follow us on Facebook, X, and YouTube by searching for Captivating History.

Table of Contents

Introduction

Without a doubt, Egypt is one of the most famous ancient civilizations in the world. Whenever we think of ancient history's greatest empires, many immediately think of Greece and Rome because of their great military campaigns, philosophers, and heroes, both historical and mythical. However, whenever Egypt is mentioned, one cannot help but immediately picture an image of Cleopatra or the Pyramid of Giza. While they are both iconic symbols of ancient Egypt, they barely scratch the surface of what Egypt truly was.

This kingdom along the Nile existed for over five thousand years. Egypt's story is more or less like a marathon rather than a sprint. Unlike Greece and Rome, which had clear beginnings, golden ages, and eventual declines, Egyptian history is far more complex. Throughout the years, there were many episodes where dynasties rose and fell, foreign rulers took the throne, resulting in the kingdom either falling into chaos or flourishing, and traditions that continued to evolve but never disappeared. Suffice it to say, but the length of the Egyptian story is astonishingly long—perhaps never-ending. Even when Cleopatra reigned, she lived closer to our present day than to the time when the first foundations of the Great Pyramid of Giza were being laid.

Of course, at the heart of the kingdom was the pharaoh. These rulers were viewed by the Egyptians as divine and the earthly embodiment of the sacred gods. These pharaohs commanded armies, commissioned grand temples, and made every decision that shaped the course of Egyptian history. Some, like Ramesses II and Hatshepsut, are still celebrated today. However, there are still many others who remain obscure or overshadowed by famous pharaohs despite their astonishing achievements or, in some cases, their bizarre reigns.

For instance, the Old Kingdom ruler, Pepi II, is known for his reign, which defied all expectations. Unlike other kings of his time, like Djoser or Khufu, who left their legacies through the construction of the Step Pyramid and the Great Pyramid of Giza, Pepi II is best known for his long reign. Typically, most Egyptian rulers sat on the throne for a few decades at most. Their lives were often cut short either by war, political intrigue, or, for those lucky enough, natural causes. However, according to ancient records, Pepi II ruled for over ninety years—some suggest sixty—earning him a place on the list of the longest monarchs in history. He wore the crown when he was only a child. While Pepi inherited a kingdom that was already flourishing, his long life also forced him to witness Egypt's power and stability gradually weakening. His later years saw the creeping decline of central authority, the rise of ambitious local governors, and the eventual fragmentation of the kingdom.

Although the names of the pharaohs are highlighted in the many books about ancient Egypt, it is impossible to dismiss that the kingdom's story is far greater than the rulers who sat on its throne. Yes, they were viewed as the earthly embodiment of the gods, but in reality, their rule depended on their thousands of subjects, from the artisans who carved and painted the walls of their tombs to the priests who maintained the grand temples and from the scribes who recorded protective hymns to the soldiers who defended Egypt's borders.

Egypt was considered a mighty empire known for its engineering and architectural wonder, wealth, trade, and successful war campaigns and invasions. However, the kingdom was not always blessed. There were times when chaos constantly loomed on the horizon. Cities were sacked, monuments were defaced, armies disappeared, and even those who built Egypt's royal tombs once laid down their tools in defiance.

Beyond the well-known tales of pharaohs and pyramids lie stories of lost structures, forgotten battles, and moments of rebellion that shook the kingdom from within. Some mysteries have lingered for millennia, while others were deliberately erased from history. This book seeks to uncover these hidden episodes and offer a clearer glimpse into a side of Egypt rarely told.

Chapter 1 – Imhotep: God or Man?

Some may have heard of the name Imhotep, perhaps through films or books that talk about the pyramids and ancient Egypt in general. Pharaohs are often remembered since their names were etched in history unless a ruler decided a past ruler should be forgotten, but there were also figures like Imhotep who contributed greatly to the ancient civilization. However, his name was seldom mentioned or even remembered by those outside the realm of Egyptology. Unlike the kings and pharaohs of Egypt, whose power was typically inherited, Imhotep was a man who earned his status through his intellect and skills.

Imhotep was not born with a silver spoon in his mouth. In fact, he lived in a rather humble village along the fertile banks of the Nile. Being born into a family of modest means, Imhotep was well aware that his path to success was not easy. He had neither connections nor privileges that could boost him up the ranks. It is well known that Egyptian society, much like every other ancient civilization in the world, had a rigid hierarchy. More often than not, birthright determined one's opportunities and fate in life.

However, there were also times when one's origin and background were put second. The ancient Egyptians also valued merit, especially in important roles tied to the kingdom and religion. Individuals with exceptional talents and skills could also have a chance to ascend the social ladder, though their path was not as straightforward compared to those with a better birthright. These people had to earn the trust of royals and court officials through their service, skill, and loyalty. Craftsmen could carve a better life if their creations and innovations were exceptional enough that they attracted the attention of the nobles, while priests could build a name for themselves if they could navigate and solve a crisis involving a god's wrath. Scribes could rise in status as well via their mastery of writing and record-keeping. Horemheb, for instance, was a royal scribe before becoming a pharaoh in the New Kingdom. As for Imhotep, he charted his course by doing nearly everything. He ventured into the worlds of architecture, religion, and administration.

Imhotep had an uncanny ability to observe the world around him. He was fascinated by the magnificent temples that dotted the kingdom. However, in his eyes, these temples were not merely places of worship. They were masterpieces that blended the sacred and the practical. Imhotep also spent his early years observing the intricate rituals performed by priests. He understood not only their symbolic meaning but also realized the ultimate precision and discipline needed to execute them.

Imhotep's first known role was that of priest of Ptah. As the creator god and patron deity of both craftsmen and architects, Ptah was highly revered in Memphis, which was also Egypt's administrative and spiritual heart at the time. Of course, in a kingdom that prioritized religion above all else, the role of a priest was a position of immense respect and authority. The responsibilities and tasks, though, were far from easy. As a priest of Ptah, Imhotep was tasked with typical religious duties, but he was also expected to preserve the sacred knowledge of architecture, medicine, and art. So, he often spent most of his time studying sacred texts in order to hone his understanding of the physical and metaphysical worlds.

His talent and devotion never went unnoticed. Imhotep was soon promoted to the position of high priest of Ptah, where he became the spiritual and intellectual leader of Memphis. With a higher position came greater responsibilities, and his role demanded rigorous devotion. He was expected to possess deep knowledge of rituals and theology, as well as the ability to manage complex temple affairs. He needed to fulfill these responsibilities, all while maintaining the favor of both the gods and the people. He was the head of elaborate religious ceremonies, but Imhotep was also the one responsible for managing the temple's extensive resources and workforce.

A depiction of Imhotep dressed in a leopard-skin robe, a ritual garment typically worn by priests.[1]

Imhotep's influence began to grow, eventually catching the attention of the reigning king, Djoser. As one of the most influential rulers of the Third Dynasty, Djoser often had his name listed as a visionary king. He sought to elevate Egypt's architectural and cultural achievements. After recognizing Imhotep's unique combination of skills, Djoser made the decision to appoint him to oversee the construction of his eternal home.

Unlike many other cultures around the globe, ancient Egyptians saw tombs as far more than just resting places for the dead. To them, tombs and burial chambers were the portals to the afterlife, a realm that was full of challenges. It was a must for these Egyptian tombs to be meticulously designed so that the deceased would be left with a safe passage for them to continue their existence in the next world.

It was clear to the ancient Egyptians that death was not the end but rather a transition to another plane of existence. However, one could only enjoy eternal life if they were given the proper rituals. For their kings especially, rituals and ceremonies were more pronounced. After all, these rulers were considered divine intermediaries, so their well-being in the afterlife was very important to maintain cosmic order. Tombs of Egyptian kings were typically constructed in the grandest way possible. Their chambers were filled with treasures and provisions, which the spirits of these kings would use during their journey through the underworld. These tombs had to be perfect to ensure the safety of the deceased kings, so the construction typically began years, if not decades, before the king's death. Djoser's decision to entrust Imhotep with this task showed the trust and respect he held for the high priest.

Long before Imhotep's innovations—or even his birth—the standard design for royal tombs was called the mastaba. Built using mudbricks, the mastaba was rectangular in shape and had flat roofs and sloping sides. This form of eternal resting place was reserved for kings and nobles. Of course, despite its simple exterior, the mastaba also featured inscriptions and carvings that typically detailed the life and achievements of the deceased.

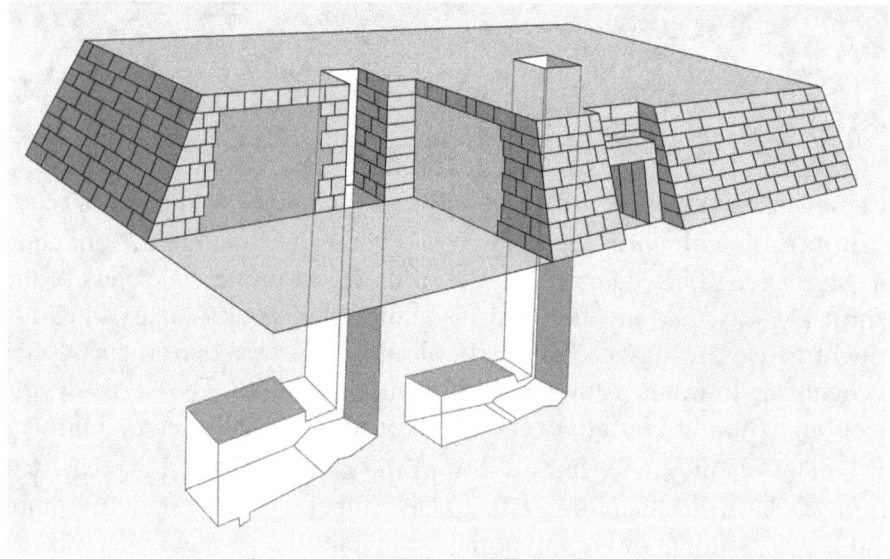

Structure of a mastaba.[2]

Interestingly, Imhotep decided to deviate from this traditional design. The reasons behind this remain a mystery, yet many agree its implications were revolutionary. Now known as the Step Pyramid, Imhotep designed Djoser's tomb with a square foundation, which was a striking difference from the mastabas, which had rectangular bases. He then stacked six mastaba-like layers on top of one another, each smaller than the one below. This allowed Imhotep to create a tower-like monument that appeared as if it was reaching for the heavens. This design presumably symbolized a divine ascent, which further reinforced the Egyptian belief that their king was connected to the gods.

Imhotep also came up with the idea of using stones to build Djoser's Step Pyramid; in the past, the Egyptians constructed tombs using mudbricks. However, despite his decision to come up with a different design, the priest and architect did not completely stray away from the traditional mastabas. Instead, he retained the old ideas but turned them into a better structure. For instance, similar to the mastabas, the pyramid complex featured walls that had patterns and little indents as decorations. He also proposed the idea of stone columns, which were carved to resemble bundles of reed and papyrus. Since the Step Pyramid was taller than its predecessors, it was crucial for Imhotep to innovate a way to ensure the pyramid never collapsed. He placed the stones at a slight inward angle, making the entire structure more stable and able to hold its own weight.

The Step Pyramid of Djoser.'

It took two decades for the builders to finally hang their tools. Upon completion, the Step Pyramid—the first Egyptian pyramid—stood proudly on the Saqqara necropolis at an astonishing height of over two hundred feet. It was the tallest structure to have ever been built at the time. The pyramid was surrounded by an impressive complex that spanned at least forty acres. Temples, courtyards, shrines, and living quarters for the priests dotted the complex, and the entire site was surrounded by a thirty-foot-high wall. A total of thirteen false doors were also installed to confuse tomb robbers. The only real entrance was built in the southeastern corner. The complex was further protected by a trench beyond the wall, which measured around 2,460 feet long and 131 feet wide.

Apart from serving as the eternal resting place for the Egyptian king (Djoser died sometime in 2649 BCE or 2611 BCE, depending on the chronology used), the Step Pyramid also became a template for future pyramids. It is safe to say that Imhotep's achievements were not just a tribute to his king but also a legacy that transformed the landscape and architecture of Egypt.

Imhotep was made Djoser's most trusted advisor. He was expected to be by the king's side during important decisions to assist him in navigating through various periods of crisis. Perhaps one of the most well-known crises during Djoser's reign was the seven-year famine that plagued the land. It all began when the Nile refused to inundate. This plunged the kingdom into complete chaos. Crops withered and refused to grow. As a kingdom that relied heavily on agriculture, it was a difficult time. Hunger spread, and many of the Egyptians resorted to robbing each other in the name of survival. Temples were closed, and shrines were no longer used.

The Famine Stela.'

According to their ancient beliefs, the annual inundation was a gift from Hapi, the god of the Nile (some scholars suggest Hapi was not a god but rather a personification of the flood itself). So, when the land failed to receive the flood for seven years straight, the Egyptians deduced that the god was somehow enraged by them. According to the Famine Stela (an ancient inscription carved centuries following the disaster), Djoser turned to Imhotep to solve the problem. He asked his advisor to search for the birthplace of Hapi himself, believing that by learning of the god's origins, he could also learn the ways to appease the god. Imhotep set out on a journey to find the answer. His first stop was the Temple of Thoth (also known as the House of the Net), where he spent hours reading through sacred texts.

His effort soon paid off. His investigation revealed that the flooding of the Nile was under the dominion of Khnum, the ram-headed god who was also believed to have created humankind on his potter's wheel. Khnum was said to have been the one who guarded the sacred spring that fed the Nile's waters. Imhotep's next step to save his people was now clear: he must journey to Elephantine, the home of the deity. Upon his arrival, Imhotep wasted no time in purifying himself before praying to Khnum. He also made offerings, hoping for the god to restore the Nile's flow and end his people's sufferings.

Perhaps exhausted from his long journey and continuous praying and rituals, Imhotep fell into a deep sleep within the sacred temple. He then dreamed of the god himself. In this dream, the mighty and kind Khnum appeared before him and spoke of his power over the Nile and the creation of life. The god promised to end the suffering of Egypt and its people by letting the waters flow once again. However, there was one condition: the Egyptians must increase their effort in worshiping the god.

When Imhotep finally awoke, he immediately recorded the details of his dream and made haste to King Djoser. The king was relieved and grateful to hear of this. Aiming to fulfill the god's demand, Djoser issued a decree to restore and enrich the Temple of Khnum. He even went to the extent of granting the temple the lands between Aswan and Tachompso. A share of imports from Nubia was also given to the temple. This way, the god would be pleased, and Egypt would be forever showered with prosperity and wealth. As if the god was pleased with the king's actions, Egypt was rewarded with the annual inundation, bringing life and abundance back to the land.

Following this episode, Imhotep's reputation continued to grow. Over time, legends and myths painted him as a figure of unparalleled wisdom who also possessed extraordinary supernatural prowess. One such record from the Tebtunis Temple Library, which dates back to the Roman period, described Imhotep as a court magician. Although heavily exaggerated and fictionalized to suit Egyptian and Roman cultural ideas, this type of narrative showed that Imhotep was regarded for a very long time, even centuries after his passing.

A seated figurine of Imhotep, possibly created during the Ptolemaic period.[5]

According to this legend, Imhotep actually had a divine lineage. His father was none other than Ptah. As a talented court magician, Imhotep was believed to have played a role in the myth of the god Osiris.

Known as the god of the afterlife, fertility, and resurrection, Osiris's most famous story begins with the betrayal of his brother, Set. Based on the myth, Osiris was a compassionate king who earned the love of his subjects. This sparked jealousy and rage within Set. So, planning to usurp the throne, Set murdered Osiris. He then dismembered his brother's body and scattered the pieces across the world.

The first rule of resurrecting a god was to ensure that he was in one piece. The myth goes on to tell how Osiris's sister-wife, Isis, retrieved Osiris's lost body parts. The records from the Tebtunis Temple Library detailed Imhotep's role in addressing this catastrophe. He was tasked with retrieving Osiris's scattered pieces. His challenging quest eventually brought him to Assyria. Here, he encountered a certain Assyrian sorceress who planned to thwart his mission. Ancient writings narrate the two confronting each other, with them using their wit and supernatural power to gain the upper hand. Imhotep ultimately emerged victorious.

The myth also narrated how Imhotep, after securing Osiris's body parts, performed sacred rites to honor and bring the god back to life. It was believed that these rites symbolized the restoration of Maat, the cosmic balance, and reaffirmed the divine authority of Osiris. With his task accomplished, Imhotep returned to Egypt, where he was celebrated as a restorer of divine harmony.

Other than the realms of myth and architecture, Imhotep was also held in high regard in the world of medicine. To this day, some acknowledge him as the first physician of the ancient world. Imhotep had been writing on the subject of medicine for over two thousand years prior to the birth of the "Father of Medicine," Hippocrates. Before Imhotep's time, Egyptian healers typically relied heavily on magic and prayers to treat illnesses. They made use of spells, charms, and incantations to help their patients. In their eyes, most diseases were caused by supernatural forces or by the patient displeasing the divine.

Imhotep, despite his pious background, embraced a more empirical approach. Although he still acknowledged the divine's work in healing, he also knew it was not enough to rely strictly on a god's intervention. Instead of using only spells and charms, he emphasized diagnosis and treatment based on careful observation. Patients were typically questioned about their symptoms, injuries, and pain. Before giving remedies, physical examinations needed to be done, which included touching, prodding, and analyzing the affected areas. This practice is reminiscent of modern medical consultations.

Imhotep is credited with diagnosing and treating perhaps as many as two hundred diseases, from tuberculosis to appendicitis and from gout, gallstones, to even arthritis. Scholars suggested that he might have had experience in performing surgeries. His techniques would not be too out of place in contemporary medical practices. This claim was further cemented by the discovery of the Edwin Smith Papyrus. Believed to be authored by Imhotep himself, this ancient text included remarkable insights into his methods and techniques. Known to be the oldest written medical document, the papyrus provided instructions for forty-eight cases of wounds, fractures, dislocations, and tumors. It also contained detailed instructions for suturing wounds and managing infections using only honey and resins.

Imhotep never planned to keep his knowledge to himself. The physician later founded the first-ever school of medicine in Memphis, where aspiring physicians often flocked to, eager to study under his guidance. His teachings and techniques undoubtedly laid the foundation for Egyptian medicine and, by extension, ensured that his legacy endured for generations.

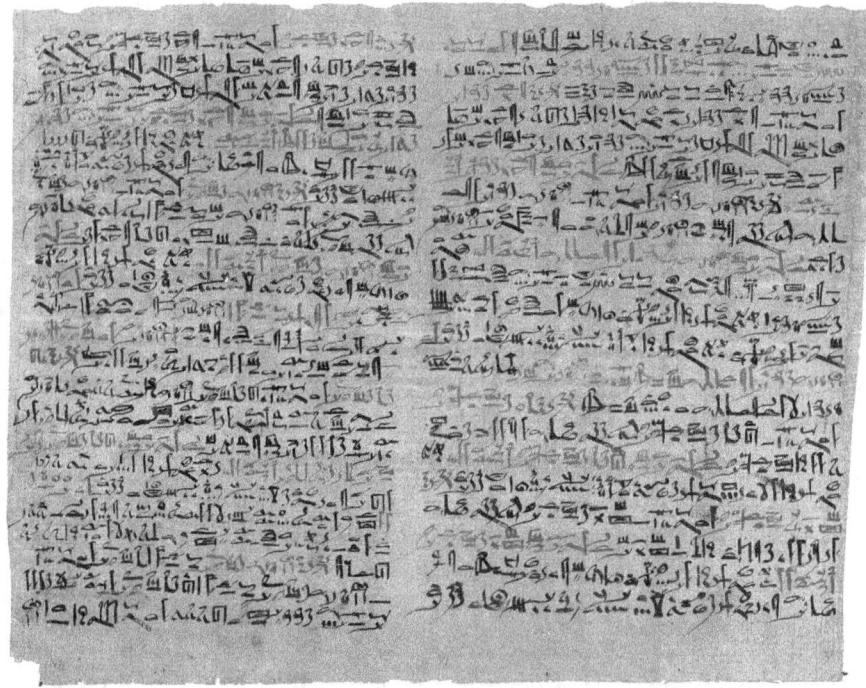

A page of the Edwin Smith Papyrus.'

Djoser was beyond impressed with Imhotep's contributions. His architectural accomplishments, in particular, were highly appreciated by the king to the point where Djoser allowed Imhotep's name to be carved alongside his own on different monuments. When the king eventually died, his remains were interred in the burial chamber right beneath the Step Pyramid, just as he had wished.

As for Imhotep, his career did not end with Djoser's departure. He was believed to have continued his service under a few more rulers of the Third Dynasty, including Sekhemkhet (c. 2650 BCE), Khaba (c. 2640 BCE), and Huni (c. 2630). However, this claim is debated by scholars. Nevertheless, Imhotep lived a remarkably long life. His talents were highly sought after for many years.

His exact year of death has yet to be confirmed. Historians and scholars believe that he lived for much of the 26th century BCE, but there are no definitive records that detail his final years.

His reputation and legacy grew stronger over time, though. When the Egyptians saw the start of the New Kingdom, Imhotep's name was still remembered. Since he was highly revered for his wisdom and mastery of written knowledge, he was eventually celebrated as a patron of scribes. So, not only did his image often appear on scribal palettes, but his name was also invoked in prayers, especially by those seeking inspiration and guidance in their works.

By the Late Period, Imhotep's legacy had been cemented. He was deified and worshiped as a god of medicine and healing. Temples dedicated to him were constructed, and there was a dedicated priesthood. His cult began on a local level in Saqqara, where he had made his greatest architectural contributions. As the years passed by, his cult expanded. His status grew beyond merely a healer to an intermediary between the divine and mortal realms. Even the Greeks, who held the Egyptian culture in high regard, acknowledged his deification. They identified Imhotep with their own god of medicine, Asclepius.

However, for someone who was once held in high esteem, it is surprising that the location of Imhotep's tomb remains one of Egypt's greatest unsolved mysteries. Just like the tombs of Alexander the Great and even Cleopatra and Mark Antony, archaeologists have never found the exact site of his tomb despite years of investigations. Only theories remain about the resting place of the man who elevated Egyptian architecture and medicine to new levels.

Theories suggest that Imhotep's tomb is located either within Djoser's burial complex or somewhere in North Saqqara, which was also the site where many significant tombs of the Third Dynasty were discovered. British archaeologist W. B. Emery, for one, conducted extensive excavations at North Saqqara. The tomb he labeled as S 3518 may be

Imhotep's final resting place. This conclusion—or speculation—was based on Emery's hypothesis about the tomb's elaborate structure. Not only did the tomb contain various votive offerings, but it also had a system of cult rooms. The most convincing evidence of all was seal imprints bearing King Djoser's name.

This conclusion has never been officially confirmed. While some scholars are open to the suggestion, others argue that Imhotep's eternal home might have been destroyed long ago. There are also historians who suggest that the tomb may have been uncovered without anyone knowing. Nevertheless, even without the discovery of his lost tomb, Imhotep succeeded in immortalizing his name. To this day, he is considered a symbol of innovation, intellect, and devotion. Many agree that he was a man ahead of his time.

Chapter 2 – Unas: The Pharaoh Who Consumed Gods

The year was 1881. There had been a new discovery at Saqqara, the vast necropolis of Egypt. Buried deep beneath the sands was a pyramid. However, unlike the grand pyramids of Giza, this one seemed rather unremarkable at first glance. Its limestone casing had long eroded, leaving the pyramid to appear as if it was nothing more than just a huge mound in the middle of the desert. However, as the team ventured into the pyramid, they uncovered something far more extraordinary. The walls of the burial chamber were adorned with rows of hieroglyphs, all carved in meticulous detail. From these inscriptions, the archaeologists learned that the pyramid was the eternal resting place for Unas, a pharaoh whose name was unfamiliar to many.

The hieroglyphs not only told the archaeologists the name of the individual buried within the tomb but also narratives of the afterlife. Known as the Pyramid Texts, these rows of hieroglyphs are today considered one of the oldest known religious writings in the world. Instead of recounting battles or listing royal titles, these walls carry a series of magic spells, hymns, and prayers meant to guide the soul of the dead pharaoh through the daunting journey across the Duat (the Egyptian underworld). They spoke of encounters with gods, battles with chaotic forces, and the ultimate union with the divine.

Pyramid Texts carved onto the walls of Unas's pyramid.'

To put it simply, the Pyramid Texts were a map to immortality. It narrated the journey of how the soul of the pharaoh would ascend to the heavens, where he would later merge with the great god of the sun, Ra. Other than the narrative of the journey, the walls of the burial chamber were also full of spells. Historians suggest that these spells served as protection for the deceased pharaohs. They were thought to have the ability to ward off serpents, demons, and other dangers lurking in the afterlife.

The ancient Egyptians were strong believers in the afterlife; they believed that death was far from the conclusion of a person's life. The journey to enjoy the next life was filled with peril and potential, even for the greatest ruler of the kingdom. However, the Pyramid Texts explain that whatever danger awaited a person in the Duat—be it a massive serpent or other vicious creatures—they could all be vanquished. One's eternal union with the gods was confirmed, given that one's tomb was adorned with such texts.

Unas, the Last King of the Fifth Dynasty

The Old Kingdom is often referred to as the golden era of pyramid building. Just as this name suggests, the period witnessed the construction of some of the most impressive monuments in human history. For centuries, the mighty pharaohs were the central figure in

Egyptian society. They were viewed as more than a king; they were seen as a living god who controlled the vast lands, economy, and military. The Old Kingdom, in particular, thrived on this model of centralized authority. Pharaohs were the ones who oversaw the construction projects and agricultural surpluses that supported the kingdom. So, whenever the construction project of a pyramid was launched, the Egyptians made sure to put a lot of effort into it. To them, the pyramids were more than just tombs for their leader; they were also grand statements of the pharaohs' divine authority.

What remains of the Pyramid of Unas.'

The Fourth Dynasty was the peak of pyramid building, with the pyramids of Giza being the most famous of all, even to this day. These tombs were so massive and built with the utmost precision that they eventually became symbols of ancient Egypt. Then, when the Egyptians saw the beginning of the Fifth Dynasty—to which Pharaoh Unas belonged—Egypt saw a slight change in the focus of its construction projects. This era was where religious innovations and the worship of Ra were more emphasized, which was why the kingdom saw more sun temples and grand complexes dedicated to the god being built.

However, these massive projects were expensive. Building such intricate structures needed a lot of workers, and the continuous demand for labor and resources eventually strained Egypt's economy. When Unas ascended the throne as the last pharaoh of the Fifth Dynasty, Egypt was still at the height of its cultural and architectural achievements. But at the same time, the kingdom was also on the brink of significant change. Egypt was facing a gradual decentralization of power.

During this time, Egypt's provinces, also referred to as nomes, were managed by nomarchs (similar to governors). Initially, these nomarchs acted as representatives of the pharaoh, but as time went by, things began to change. The nomarchs gradually accumulated wealth and authority over the years, and they began to stray away from the central government. By the time Unas wore the crown, the balance of power was already shifting away from the pharaoh. Combined with Egypt's economic challenges, the times when monumental pyramids dotted the land had ended. The Pyramid of Unas at Saqqara reflected this change; it was significantly smaller than those that housed his predecessors.

Nevertheless, Egypt under Unas remained a powerful kingdom. Despite its economy being strained, the kingdom was still supported by flourishing trade networks. The pharaoh's mortuary temple featured evidence of this; archaeologists have discovered reliefs that depict Unas launching trade missions to Punt, a mysterious land renowned for its precious and invaluable resources, such as incense, myrrh, ebony, gold, and an array of exotic animals. There were also inscriptions that talked about military campaigns into Canaan or Nubia during his reign. Scholars debate the details of these campaigns—some claim they were more symbolic than factual—but these inscriptions portrayed the traditional image of the pharaoh as both a powerful warrior and the protector of the realm.

Although his pyramid and mortuary temple were considered modest in scale, these structures appeared as if they were constructed by the most skilled craftsmen in the kingdom. It is safe to assume that Unas's administration, despite its challenges, was still capable of mobilizing talented artisans. Other reliefs from his temple featured scenes of daily life, agricultural abundance, and various religious rituals. These images offer us a glimpse into the society he once ruled.

Unas's reign also marked a turning point in the realm of religion. Although Ra remained the central figure of the Egyptian pantheon, Osiris, the god of the underworld and resurrection, rose in influence. Osiris represented a shift in focus from the solar deities to those associated with death, renewal, and the afterlife. Perhaps it was this change that drove Unas to introduce the first-ever Pyramid Texts.

Unas's Pyramid Complex

The pharaoh's pyramid was built sometime in 2375 BCE. During its golden age, the structure stood at a height of forty-three meters. However, when erosion struck the structure many centuries later, Unas's once-grand pyramid was reduced to only a weathered mound of rubble. However, this state was only on its exterior; the pyramid's interior and its surrounding complex still is mostly intact.

Believe it or not, Unas's pyramid was the first to feature inscriptions in its burial chamber, which set it apart from its predecessors. True, the ancient Egyptians were always known for their innovations and creativity, especially when it came to architecture. However, the decorations in this specific pyramid brought their skills to a whole new level, especially since it was constructed over four thousand years ago. The walls of the chamber were lined with polished white alabaster, invoking a sense of elegance, and the contrasting hieroglyphs painted with blue pigment further added to the chamber's intricacy. One can only imagine the ethereal look of the chamber when it was freshly constructed.

The main highlight of the chamber was the Pyramid Texts, which transformed the pyramid from a mere tomb into a spiritual sanctuary. The walls were not the only ones adorned with inscriptions and images. Above, the chamber's ceiling was painted with golden stars set against a dark background. Scholars suggested that the dark background symbolized the night sky, with the stars representing the gods as well as the pharaoh himself, who was thought to have earned a place among the celestial beings.

The restored causeway at Unas's pyramid complex.'

The pyramid complex also featured a causeway, which is easily comparable to the one at Khufu's Pyramid. Stretching almost 750 meters from the pyramid's eastern side to the valley temple, the causeway was initially roofed, and its walls were heavily decorated with reliefs depicting an array of scenes, from agricultural activities to trade expeditions to religious rituals. The most intriguing image along the causeway shows a rather dark scene. The humans appeared emaciated. Scholars interpreted this as evidence of a famine that struck the Egyptians during Unas's reign. This relief was unique, as it contrasted with the usual depictions of abundance and prosperity, providing us with a rare peek into the misfortune faced by the kingdom. Unfortunately, the majority of the causeway is now in ruins. However, archaeologists were able to save portions of its reliefs, such as the images of famine. These are now preserved in the Imhotep Museum, which is located nearby.

Interestingly, to the south of the upper causeway, one can find two boat pits. Measuring about forty-five meters long each, these pits were designed to hold wooden ceremonial boats. Although these boats have long since disappeared, historians suggest that back then, these boats were probably viewed as a symbol of Ra's solar barque, which the sun god sailed in during his journey through the sky and the Duat.

The pyramid complex also boasted a bustling necropolis. To this day, over two hundred tombs have been excavated in the vicinity. The tombs of Unas's queens were also uncovered, along with other prominent officials of the Fifth and Sixth Dynasties. While two of Unas's queens, Nebet and Khenut, were buried in a double mastaba near the pyramid, his daughter Princess Idut's tomb was adorned with beautifully preserved carvings and paintings. Not far from Unas's eternal home were also the tombs of Mehu, the royal vizier from the Sixth Dynasty, and Nefer, whose titles included the supervisor of artisans and director of choir singers. Similarly, both of their tombs featured images of courtly life and religious practices during Unas's time.

The Cannibal Hymn, a Collection of Inscriptions That Sparked Controversies

Perhaps the most startling feature of the Pyramid Texts carved onto the walls of Unas's burial chamber is the Cannibal Hymn. This inscription was popular for its vivid yet unsettling imagery. The hymn describes a deceased king who had been deified engaging in an act of cannibalism. Instead of eating the flesh of mortals, though, the deified king is devouring the gods themselves to absorb their powers and assert his supremacy in the divine realm.

Historians agree that the Cannibal Hymn is unique; it is known for its obvious divergence from the more orderly and serene imagery typically associated with Egyptian funerary texts. While other spells included in the typical Pyramid Texts often focused on harmony, purification, and the journey to eternal peace, this specific hymn showed a far more aggressive vision of the pharaoh's afterlife. The hymn pictured the pharaoh as a conqueror not only on earth but also in the celestial realm, where he had to assert his place among the divine through acts of symbolic violence and assimilation.

However, the discovery of this dark inscription has sparked debates among the scholars and historians who have sought to interpret the meaning of the hymn. While many scholars agree that the hymn is symbolic, some have proposed controversial ideas about its origins and meaning. Ernest Alfred Wallis Budge, for instance, proposed one such theory. This early 20th-century Egyptologist earned his reputation through his work on various ancient Egyptian texts, including the famed Papyrus of Ani (also known as the Book of the Dead). In 1911, the Egyptologist authored his book called *Osiris and the Egyptian Resurrection*, in which he suggested that the Osiris myth—and, by extension, the Cannibal Hymn—was purposely created by the early Egyptians to discourage cannibalistic practices. Budge suggested that the image from the Cannibal Hymn, where the pharaoh consumed gods to gain their power, actually symbolized the practice of consuming human flesh. To eliminate this practice altogether, the state priests of the Old Kingdom invented the story of Osiris's death and resurrection to introduce the practice of mummification. This was thought to replace the practice of cannibalism, ensuring that bodies were preserved in the best condition possible rather than being consumed.

Although the theory initially gained some traction, it has been largely dismissed. Later scholars had trouble finding conclusive evidence that cannibalism was ever practiced by the ancient Egyptians, be it ritually or otherwise. The Cannibal Hymn is now believed to have been nothing more than a metaphor; it simply symbolized the pharaoh's ultimate dominance over his realm and his divine nature.

Another renowned Egyptologist, Miriam Lichtheim, also proposed a theory that focused more on the hymn's political and symbolic themes. According to Lichtheim, the phrases in the hymn that described Unas "eating the Red" and "swallowing the Green" are not references to flesh and blood like many others suggested. Instead, it was actually a metaphor symbolizing the unification of Upper and Lower Egypt. The word "Red" could refer to the Red Crown of Lower Egypt, while "Green" might have symbolized the Wadjet, the cobra goddess of Upper Egypt. Therefore, by depicting the pharaoh consuming these symbols, it meant that Unas was the ultimate ruler of the two lands.

Last but not least, the hymn can also be seen as part of the theological innovations of the Fifth Dynasty, a time when the pharaoh's connection to Ra was increasingly emphasized. Scholars have suggested that despite the Cannibal Hymn's aggressive imagery, the meaning behind it probably was far from how it looked. The inscriptions might have symbolized the king's triumph over chaos, with the imagery of the pharaoh consuming the gods simply meaning he had assimilated with the deities, becoming a unifying cosmic force. Instead of an act of destruction, the inscription might be talking about transformation and integration.

Ancient Egypt after Unas's Departure

After the death of Unas, the ancient Egyptians saw the end of the Fifth Dynasty. While his predecessors had their legacies tied to sun temples and pyramids the size of enormous mountains, Unas left behind a different kind of legacy—one that was rooted in innovation rather than scale. It is safe to say that his reign marked a period of transition, where the focus shifted from outward displays of power to the deeper spiritual needs of the afterlife.

The political landscape of the kingdom during the time of his reign was also growing more complex. As the years passed by, the pharaoh's authority was chipped away bit by bit by the nomarchs who controlled the nomes. This was not an immediate crisis, but the gradual decentralization of the government set in motion the eventual fragmentation of the Old Kingdom. Although the kingdom was still unified when Unas left the world, the balance of power was already tilting. The nomarchs, who continued to expand their wealth and influence, soon created a network of regional power centers that would challenge the authority of the pharaohs of the Sixth Dynasty.

Unas was succeeded by Teti, the first ruler of the Sixth Dynasty. Records are scarce, but historians are confident that his ascension to power went smoothly. Under Teti's watchful eyes, the Egyptians continued many of the traditions established during the Fifth Dynasty. Pyramids continued to be constructed, and the Egyptians also placed emphasis on religious practices involving Ra and Osiris. However, the pyramids constructed during this period became increasingly modest due to the kingdom's economic constraints.

Nevertheless, the practice of including Pyramid Texts in burial chambers continued to be adopted and expanded by later kings. Initially, the funerary texts were reserved only for the royals, but later on, these inscriptions also were etched on the walls of tombs belonging to non-royal elites. When Egypt entered the era of the Middle Kingdom, the Pyramid Texts went through an evolution. The Coffin Texts were also used by commoners. Instead of being inscribed on the walls of burial chambers, the Coffin Texts were typically painted on the inside of coffins—hence the name. This way, even the most ordinary citizens could gain the same protections and guidance in the afterlife. Although resurrection, purification, and cosmic unity remained the central theme of these texts, not every spell appeared the same. They were also adjusted and personalized to fit different individuals.

The Pyramid Texts were the foundation for the creation of the Book of the Dead, which first emerged during the New Kingdom. This funerary text was often written on papyrus scrolls and buried with the deceased. Similar to its precursor, the scrolls also featured spells, incantations, rituals, and prayers to overcome the hurdles thrown to the deceased in the Duat. The only difference was that it was in a more portable format. The most famous of this text is the Papyrus of Ani, which was discovered in 1888. This scroll, which is full of cursive hieroglyphs, is considered the finest, best-preserved, and most detailed Egyptian funerary text to ever exist.

Chapter 3 – The Mystery of the Sea Peoples

The Late Bronze Age (c. 1600–1200 BCE) was a period of prosperity and interconnectedness. Powerful kingdoms of the ancient Mediterranean, such as the Egyptians, the Hittites, and the Mycenaeans, grew tremendously. While these kingdoms clashed swords with each other from time to time, warfare was not constant. More often than not, diplomacy was practiced, useful innovations were shared, and precious goods were traded with each other. Cyprus, for instance, was known for its copper, while the Levant (the modern-day areas of Lebanon and Syria) had plenty of cedar trees. The Egyptians, on the other hand, were rich in gold. Much of this precious mineral, however, was extracted from Nubia, a region under Egyptian control during the New Kingdom. These goods moved across vast distances, allowing these kingdoms to achieve even greater heights as time passed by.

Of course, ancient Egypt, under the New Kingdom pharaohs, was the center of this interconnected world. The Egyptians peaked as early as the 13th century BCE, with their kingdom stretching from Nubia in the south to Canaan in the north. Egypt's influence grew even more following the reign of Ramesses II. The kingdom did not only see territorial expansion but also major growth in its economy and culture. It is safe to conclude that the pharaohs of the New Kingdom emphasized diplomatic efforts. The Amarna Letters are evidence of this; the preserved documents revealed a world of royal alliances and rivalries where gifts were often exchanged between rulers in order to ensure peace or leverage power.

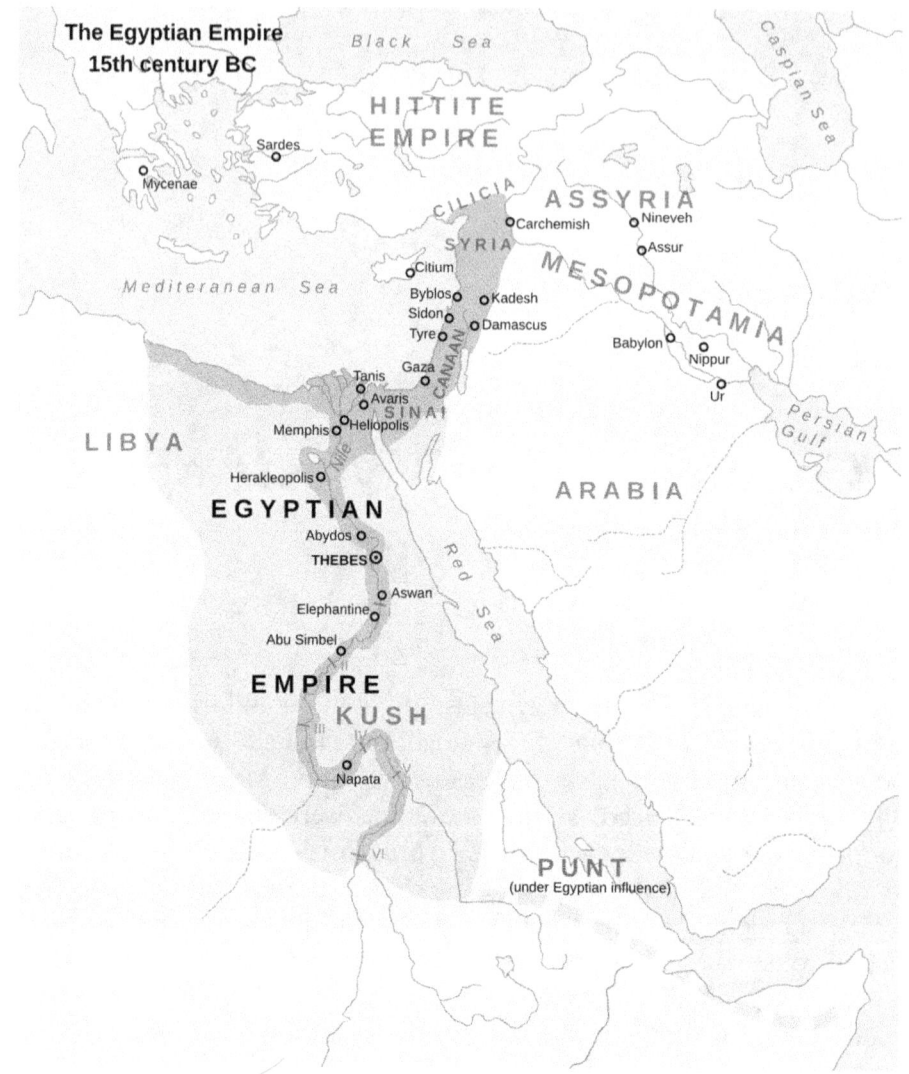

The Egyptian Empire
15th century BC

Egyptian territories during the New Kingdom period.[11]

Meanwhile, the Hittite Empire based in Anatolia (modern-day Turkey) was also growing into a formidable empire. With control over vital trade routes that linked the eastern Mediterranean to the lands of the Near East, the Hittites were able to gain immense wealth and resources. But, of course, this dominance also caused problems. Conflicts were brewing on the horizon, and the Hittites eventually turned into one of Egypt's greatest rivals. These two powers vied for control over Canaan. Their rivalry reached a climax in the Battle of Kadesh, which erupted in 1274 BCE. This was the bloody episode where the

Egyptian pharaoh, Ramesses II, faced the Hittite king, Muwatalli II. Despite being known as one of the most famous battles of the ancient world, the Battle of Kadesh ended in a stalemate.

However, wars and battles were not the only things that exposed the vulnerabilities of kingdoms. While trade routes brought wealth to these ancient civilizations, they could just as easily spread instability when they were disrupted. The Egyptians enjoyed an era of prosperity, but they were not free from obstacles. Maintaining such a massive empire required substantial effort. Immense resources and a well-trained military were needed to ensure its borders and secure trade routes from impending threats. Rebellions were still a common occurrence during this time, and there were also foreign threats spearheaded by those driven by the tantalizing wealth of the kingdom.

Egypt also had to deal with its own internal issues. Succession in Egypt was not always smooth, and there were multiple times when the kingdom struggled with the inconsistent inundation of the Nile. Mother Nature has never been known for her mercy. Ancient Egypt was not the only kingdom to have experienced her wrath; cities like Ugarit (an ancient port city in northern Syria), for example, were terrorized by earthquakes, leaving them vulnerable and an easy target for invaders. Back then, rulers relied on complex, centralized governments to keep order. However, as their territories grew, these kingdoms also saw the rise of local rulers who began acting on their own. This decentralized governing structure undoubtedly weakened the unity of great powers like Egypt and the Hittite Empire, thus leaving the door open for invaders to strike.

The first signs of trouble could be seen by the late 13th century BCE. Reports of raids constantly came in from coastal cities that had long thrived in the region. Interestingly, these cities were unfamiliar with the groups that launched these vicious raids. Following these attacks, trade networks began to falter, and many settlements that had once enjoyed prosperity were silenced. Later known as the Sea Peoples, these groups moved swiftly across the Mediterranean, their raids shaking the very foundations of the Late Bronze Age world. Perhaps united and driven by either necessity or opportunism, they would soon be a destructive force that would challenge even the might of Egypt.

The Origin of the Sea Peoples

According to ancient records, the Sea Peoples arrived in waves. They often raided coastal settlements, toppled cities, and disrupted the vast trade networks that had existed for centuries. However, up to this day, the exact origins of these peoples remain one of the most hotly debated topics of the ancient world.

The term "Sea Peoples" came from Egyptian records, particularly the inscriptions found at Medinet Habu. This grand temple was built by the second pharaoh of the Twentieth Dynasty, Ramesses III. Here, scholars discovered inscriptions that detailed dramatic scenes of battles where the Egyptians fought against invaders arriving in ships. These inscriptions tell us of the great struggle the Egyptians were facing, yet they fail to tell us exactly where the Sea Peoples came from. However, scholars and historians agree that the Sea Peoples were not a single unified army but rather a confederation of different groups united by necessity, ambition, or perhaps both.

An inscription at Medinet Habu depicting Ramesses III going against the Sea Peoples at the Battle of the Delta.[13]

One theory suggests that the Sea Peoples came from the Aegean world, particularly from the Mycenaean civilization. They were once the mightiest in the region. Having built grand palace-states in Mycenae, Pylos, and Tiryns, the Mycenaeans controlled a vast trade network that spread across the region. Unfortunately, something went awfully wrong. The civilization found itself in a steep decline by the late 13th century BCE. Centuries of excavations found traces of their fall. Palaces were burned to the ground, trade routes vanished, and the Linear B script (the writing system of the Mycenaean civilization) disappeared. What truly caused the downfall of the Mycenaeans remains a debate, yet we can be sure that when their world collapsed, its people had no other choice but to flee. It is plausible that these displaced Mycenaeans made use of their knowledge of seafaring and maritime trade routes to survive. Of course, they did so not as merchants but as formidable raiders whose targets were vulnerable coastal settlements.

Another theory states that the Sea Peoples came from Anatolia, particularly its western coastal regions like Lukka (ancient Lycia). Due to internal revolts and external threats, the Hittite Empire was struggling during the Late Bronze Age. Records from the capital city of Hattusa described this unrest, indicating that the western provinces, in particular, were unstable. Shifting alliances were normal, and rebellions constantly erupted. Perhaps because of these episodes of hardship, which included economic problems, war, and even famine, the people of these regions eventually chose to leave their homeland. Scholars suggest that they then joined the growing confederation of the Sea Peoples. The Lukka were also mentioned in the Egyptian inscriptions, which possibly links them to the maritime incursions into Egypt by the Sea Peoples.

The Egyptians also mentioned other names of groups of the Sea Peoples. There were the Peleset (possibly the same as the Philistines), the Sherden, the Shekelesh, and the Denyen. According to Ramesses III's inscriptions, these groups were the ones who attacked Egypt on both land and sea. They were portrayed as a fearsome and organized force. However, out of all these groups, the mention of the Sherden opens the door to yet another theory surrounding the Sea Peoples' origins.

The Sherden were described by the ancient Egyptians to be fierce warriors who went into battle wearing horned helmets and armed with round shields. Interestingly and strangely enough, archaeologists found similar helmets in Sardinia. This suggests that the Sea Peoples might have come from the western Mediterranean. However, this finding did not entirely answer the question. Yes, the Sherden might have come from Sardinia, but there is also the possibility that they were simply influenced by the warrior traditions of that region.

Regardless of the answer, it is safe to conclude that the Sea Peoples were a mix of different groups, possibly hailing from different parts of the Mediterranean. The reason behind their unity might have been due to displacement caused by either natural disasters, famine, or societal collapse. These groups possibly shared the same goal, which was to search for new opportunities—or rather survival—amidst the backdrop of the tumultuous Late Bronze Age.

The Sea Peoples vs. the Ancient Egyptians

The Egyptians experienced their first encounter against the Sea Peoples decades before the rise of Ramesses III. Their earliest known confrontation could be traced back to the early 13th century when Pharaoh Merneptah (the successor of Ramesses II) sat on the throne. It was forever immortalized on the Stela of Merneptah (inscribed in 1208 BCE), which recalls an episode where a coalition of Libyan tribes and the Sea Peoples attempted to invade Egypt from the west.

It began when the Libyans had grown desperate due to the periods of drought and famine. With food and water becoming increasingly harder to come by, they had no other choice but to seek better lands. The fertile Nile Valley and its rich resources became their prime target. However, to go against such a powerful kingdom, the Libyans needed help. This was when the Sea Peoples (the groups listed on the Merneptah Stele were the Ekwesh, Shekelesh, Lukka, Sherden, and Teresh) came into play. Together, the Libyans and the Sea Peoples pushed toward the Nile Delta. The sheer size of the coalition, combined with the Sea Peoples' exceptional naval and military expertise, made the invasion a significant threat.

Merneptah wasted no time in responding to the invasion. After amassing his army, the pharaoh met the invaders in battle. According to the stela, the Egyptians were blessed with a resounding victory. Thousands of the Sea Peoples and their Libyan allies were annihilated. Those who were lucky enough to survive ended up captured with no hope of ever tasting freedom again. Of course, it is worth noting that the stela was heavily propagandistic. Yes, Merneptah succeeded in defeating the Sea Peoples, who were already thought to be a major force in the Mediterranean at the time. Yet, the pharaoh's victory only secured Egypt's borders for a temporary period.

The Sea Peoples soon showed their might once more, as they were headstrong in defeating their Egyptian enemies. They launched their most audacious campaigns when Egypt was put under the control of Ramesses III. By 1177 BCE, the Egyptians had begun to increasingly feel the suffering caused by the many raids orchestrated by the Sea

Peoples. They launched coordinated assaults by land and sea. They wreaked havoc on multiple cities. Scenes of the Battle of Djahy, fought in the northeastern Levant, and the Battle of the Delta, fought on the eastern Nile Delta, were both recorded in the reliefs carved at the temple of Medinet Habu.

The Battle of Djahy, which was fought on land, was considered the first significant engagement of this big campaign. Due to its location in the northern region of Canaan, Djahy was known to be a critical gateway to Egypt's borders. Therefore, it made sense for the Sea Peoples to shift their focus to this area after successfully devastating several cities across the eastern Mediterranean. They had even succeeded in sacking the Hittite vassal of Amurru, which was located a short distance away from the border of Egypt.

Based on the intricate reliefs at Medinet Habu, the battle was beyond chaotic. Brutality immediately took over as Ramesses III's forces engaged the invaders. However, the Egyptians had an advantage: their knowledge of the terrain. They knew exactly where to establish fortified positions that could slow the enemy's advance. We could say that the Egyptians' morale was through the roof since their own pharaoh was leading them in battle—at least according to the reliefs, which feature the pharaoh at the forefront. The Egyptians, from archers to charioteers to infantry, struck at the Sea Peoples, eventually driving them into disarray. Blood continued to stain the battlefield as the Egyptians advanced.

Once again, the Sea Peoples were defeated. They failed to break through Egypt's northeastern defenses, but they never planned on retreating entirely. With their plan to penetrate the kingdom by land foiled, the Sea Peoples chose to launch a naval assault on the Nile Delta next. Known simply as the Battle of the Delta, this is seen as another one of the most famous clashes to take place during Ramesses III's reign; it was second only to the previous Battle of Djahy.

The reliefs at Medinet Habu portrayed the Sea Peoples' fleet as an imposing force. Perhaps using their expertise to navigate the sea, they could cut swiftly through the treacherous eastern Mediterranean waters. While papyrus-reed boats were commonly used on the Nile, the Sea Peoples were believed to have arrived in vessels with sturdy wooden hulls and high curved prows and stern. This particular design was typically seen on Aegean and Near Eastern ships. They were better suited for navigating rough sea waves, making them well suited for long-distance open-sea voyages. One of the most interesting features of their vessels was the bird-head decorations. Historians and scholars still debate the exact meaning behind this design, but since they bore similarities to Aegean and Mycenaean ship decorations, it might suggest these Sea Peoples had ties to those regions. Aboard these vessels were warriors who were armed with javelins, swords, and round shields. According to the reliefs, some of them also wore helmets adorned with plumes and horns.

Ramesses III was well aware of the Sea Peoples' naval prowess. He was not intimidated by it since the Egyptians had already experienced their fair share of naval battles. Relying on Egyptian intelligence (the pharaoh had scouts, and his people intercepted communications), the Egyptians were able to anticipate the Sea Peoples' movements. To prepare for the impending battle, the pharaoh placed ships—all of which were smaller compared to those of their enemies but still highly maneuverable—along the Nile. The spots were meticulously chosen so that they could gain the full geographical advantage of the river.

When it was time for the confrontation, the Egyptian vessels did not hesitate to ram the Sea Peoples' ships. They splintered their hulls, resulting in the warriors falling into the Nile. Egyptian archers, who were stationed on the decks, unleashed volleys of arrows toward their enemies. This created chaos and undoubtedly affected the morale of the remaining invaders.

The Egyptians were also successful in repelling the Sea Peoples who had managed to disembark. Ramesses III himself was said to have spearheaded the charge. A relief of the pharaoh in his war chariot, bow drawn, can be seen on the wall of his mortuary temple. The Sea Peoples fought with their full might, but their skills were no match for the Egyptians. In the end, many of their warriors were killed or captured. Those who managed to escape made their way back to their shattered ships.

These battles had caused destruction across the lands. Egypt had to use its already draining resources to rebuild its defenses and protect its frontiers. Yet, the kingdom persisted, and it would eventually get back on its feet, flourishing for many centuries to come. However, the same could not be said for other civilizations across the Mediterranean. The Sea Peoples left a path of destruction across the region the moment they disembarked from their ships. They toppled cities, disrupted trade, and, by extension, became the catalyst for the decline of some of the greatest powers of the Late Bronze Age.

Coastal hubs like Ugarit once enjoyed peace and stability, serving as the center of trade and culture on the Mediterranean until the arrival of the Sea Peoples. Letters have been unearthed that give us a glimpse into the city's last days. Ugarit sent desperate pleas to its allies, hoping reinforcements would arrive and repel the invaders, but unfortunately, they were all left unanswered. The city eventually had its defenses overwhelmed by the Sea Peoples, resulting in its complete abandonment later on. Alashiya (modern Cyprus) faced an almost similar fate. Known for its copper production, it is not surprising that Alashiya was included in the Sea Peoples' list of targets. Historians suggest that upon disrupting the kingdom's trade networks, the Sea Peoples laid waste to its many settlements. Even the Hittite Empire was not spared. By the time of the Sea Peoples' emergence, the empire was already struggling because of internal strife and resource shortages. The Sea Peoples were quick to notice this, so they laid attacks on the empire's western territories. Their actions eventually contributed to the downfall of the once mighty empire's capital, Hattusa.

The collapse of these cities not only affected their populations. In fact, it caused a ripple effect across the Mediterranean since the trade networks were disrupted. These networks were the very thing that kept these civilizations connected. Through these networks, the exchange of goods was made possible. Copper and tin (both crucial components of bronze), timber, grain, and other luxury items like gold and ivory flowed through the cities in the region, allowing them to grow and thrive. However, following the raids of the Sea Peoples and their disruption of the trade routes, these cities were unable to obtain the resources they needed. This plunged them into an economic crisis, which, in time, contributed to instability and the displacement of the population.

At a glance, the movements of the Sea Peoples left destruction across the region. However, after looking closely, scholars suggest that their arrival might have contributed to the transition of the Iron Age (c. 1200-1000 BCE). With the disruption of trade networks and the collapse of major cities that produced bronze, such as Hattusa and Ugarit, societies of the region were left with only the choice of turning to iron. Other historians and scholars suggest that the Sea Peoples might have played a role in spreading iron-smelting techniques after adopting them from regions they had previously settled in. This could be seen in Philistine cities, which had early iron artifacts following the arrival of the Sea Peoples.

The Sea Peoples Following Their Defeat against the Egyptians

The Sea Peoples were primarily known for their destruction and invasions. Records of their raids were plentiful, yet none talked about what exactly happened to them in later years. Mentions of the Sea Peoples more or less vanished from the historical records, especially following their final defeat with Egypt. It is safe to assume that they did not all disappear. They likely integrated into local societies.

One of the groups of the Sea Peoples, Peleset, might have settled in Canaan years following the disastrous campaign in Egypt. They soon became known as the Philistines. This theory is further supported by archaeological findings in sites like Ashkelon, Gaza, and Ekron. Here, Mycenaean-style pottery was unearthed, along with unique architectural styles and dietary practices that were fairly similar to those of the Peleset.

Other groups, such as the Sherden and Shekelesh, did not leave a clear trace of what happened to them. It is plausible that they were absorbed into the societies they had once wreaked havoc upon. Scholars suggest that the Sherden mercenaries were integrated into Egypt, where they served the pharaoh as mercenaries. The Lukka might have integrated into smaller, localized communities or other emerging powers. The rest of the groups likely saw their identities dissolve over the generations as they assimilated into the broader cultures of the regions they chose to settle.

As for Egypt, the chaos that came with the Sea Peoples forced them to adapt and evolve. Indeed, they were victorious against the Sea Peoples, but there was always the possibility of more invasions happening, be it by the Sea Peoples or other rising forces. Because of this, the Egyptians began to work on some changes, hoping they would repeat their victory if they were ever faced with another threat.

Despite not being able to emerge unscathed, Egypt's ability to respond quickly and avoid the chaos of the Late Bronze Age from devouring them whole undoubtedly cemented its reputation as one of the most enduring and powerful civilizations of the ancient world.

Chapter 4 – Unveiling the Secrets of Deir el-Medina

The sun had just risen, bringing with it a whole new day. Its rays hit the mudbrick homes of Deir el-Medina, making these structures appear as if they were constructed in gold. This village was nestled between rugged hills and had long been the home of the kingdom's most skilled craftsmen. However, these were no ordinary workers. The inhabitants of Deir el-Medina were the artisans entrusted with building the royal tombs of the Valley of the Kings.

For one particular artisan in the village—let us refer to him as Bakennu—his day began with a ritual. In his humble house, Bakennu had a shrine that was carved into the wall. Before stepping out of his house, the thirty-year-old artisan would pause in front of the shrine, where a small painted figure of Ptah (the ancient Egyptian god of craftsman) stood proudly. He would murmur prayers, hoping the god would grant him safety throughout the day. Bakennu then placed a small offering before the god, usually a piece of bread and water. Only then would the artisan step out of his abode, making his way to work. To Bakennu, it was his duty to finish the construction of the royal tombs, while to others, it was a privilege or a burden.

Although it was still early in the morning, the atmosphere of Deir el-Medina was already alive. The narrow streets were filled with people carrying out their daily activities. Women could be seen carrying baskets of grain, which they would grind into flour. Others wove linens before heading home later in the evening, where they would prepare food for the family. Scribes, holding wooden tablets that they used to take account of the day's work, hastily made their way along the streets. Children ran between houses, their laughter often putting a smile on the faces of the adults. This was a typical scene in the village, which had existed for generations.

What remains of the houses that once belonged to the workers at Deir el-Medina.[18]

As for Bakennu, the artisan was always accompanied by a few other workers who would take the same trek into the valley. All of them carried their tools wrapped in cloth. One was a stonecutter, whose responsibility was to shape the foundations of the tombs and ensure each chamber of the tomb was carved in precise alignment. If he were to mess up even the smallest calculation, the entire structure could crumble in a matter of seconds. Bakennu was a painter. His main task was to bring life to the walls of the tombs. He was exceptionally skilled in painting depictions of the gods and scenes of divine judgment and the pharaoh's own journey into the afterlife.

Once the workers had arrived at the worksite, they immediately gathered around in a shaded alcove. Here, their overseer would be waiting for them. In his hands were a tablet and a reed pen. The overseer, who was also a scribe, recorded everything, from the hours worked to the tools borrowed to which craftsmen were there that day.

After the short meeting, Bakennu wasted no time and began to work. He took his place in one of the newly constructed tomb chambers and looked at the undercoat of plaster that had been applied to the smoothened limestone walls just a few days before. To his eyes, this was more than just a wall; it was an empty canvas, waiting to be filled with colorful paintings of the great pharaoh making offerings to Ra, Osiris, and other gods.

The Valley of the Kings.[14]

Bakennu then reached for his reed brush and dipped it into a pot of red ochre. With flair, he began drawing the outline of a figure. He had been painting ever since he could remember, so his hand was very steady. Hours passed by, and the simple outline had transformed into a painting of a pharaoh on his chariot.

Bakennu was not the only painter there. Another, just as talented as him, could be seen working with ground malachite, which he used to add a shade of green to the depiction of the papyrus fields of the afterlife. A few steps away from him was another painter who was crushing lapis lazuli to create the deep blue that would fill the starry ceiling above the burial chamber. These painters knew every detail of their work was essential, especially when these depictions were meant to last an eternity.

Some might say it was quiet work, but at the same time, it was far from silent. Coming from a different tomb from where Bakennu was, faint yet steady sounds of chisels tapping the rock could be heard. The chisels carved away the walls bit by bit as carvers inscribed the hymns from the Book of the Dead. Like the painters, their task was equally crucial; these hymns would guide the deceased pharaohs through the obstacles of the underworld. Without them, it was impossible for the spirit of these pharaohs to unite with the divine.

When the sun hung high in the sky, signaling it was time for lunch, the workers dropped their tools and took their well-earned rest. Sitting under the shade of an overhanging rock, Bakennu and his friends unwrapped the meals prepared by their wives. They enjoyed flatbread, onions, and dried fish. They quenched their thirst with cool water, which was stored in clay jars. Of course, this recess was not only reserved for eating. While enjoying their meals, Bakennu and the others would talk. Some spoke of the pharaoh's recent victories, while others grumbled about their wages and complained about the price of grain.

They continued working afterward, filling the hours with careful brush strokes and precise carvings. It was only when the sun's rays began to fade that they knew the day had almost come to an end. The overseer would give the final call when the sun had dipped behind the rugged cliffs. With the day's work done, Bakennu and the others packed their tools and wrapped them securely in cloth before making the journey back home.

As he stepped into his home, Bakennu was welcomed with a pleasant scent; his wife had been simmering lentils and roasting a goat for dinner. After greeting her husband, Bakennu's wife set out the meal and called for their children. They ate as a family and told each other all the things that had happened in their day. Later that night, Bakennu made sure to perform yet another ritual. He walked to the small temple located at the edge of the village, where he left another offering to the gods. His work on the Valley of the Kings was far from done, so Bakennu knew he would need all the blessings and protection the gods could offer him.

The routine was repeated the following day and the next until the tombs were done and another pharaoh sat on the throne, commissioning yet another grand project. As long as the pharaohs continued to rule Egypt, the inhabitants of Deir-el Medina would always have work to do.

The Early Days of Deir el-Medina

The ancient Egyptians were always known for their belief in life after death. It was important for them to be well prepared for the underworld since the journey was known to be fraught with perils. While the commoners wished to simply be granted peace when they reached the Field of Reeds (similar to the concept of paradise in other religious beliefs), the pharaohs, in particular, sought not just to reign during their lives but also after their deaths.

In order to achieve such a dream, these rulers had to ensure their tombs were filled with goods. And to ensure these goods remained safe from the hands of greedy criminals, their tombs had to be hidden away in the cliffs of Thebes. Later known as the Valley of the Kings, this site of hidden rock-cut tombs was a stark contrast to the burial traditions of the Old and Middle Kingdoms. These two periods saw the construction of massive pyramid tombs out in the open, while the ones in the Valley of the Kings appeared unassuming from the exterior yet extremely lavish on the inside.

Of course, these grand tombs would not build themselves. The pharaohs needed artisans, but not those who were untrained. They required the most skilled craftsmen the kingdom could offer, men who had mastered the art of stonecutting, sculpture, and painting. These men were expected to transform rock into a sacred passage to the afterlife, ensuring their pharaohs could achieve eternal life.

Deir el-Medina began to take shape. This walled village had its initial foundations laid during the early years of the Eighteenth Dynasty, most likely when Thutmose I (c. 1506-1493 BCE)—some suggest it was Thutmose III (1479-1425 BCE)—sat on the throne. Since this was where the permanent workforce would call home, the construction of the village was meticulously planned. Not only was it enclosed by high walls to protect the village from the dangers of the desert, but Deir el-Medina was also positioned far from the bustling city. It was located in a desert valley west of Thebes, right in between the Valley of the Kings and the Valley of the Queens. Despite being secluded, the village was still close enough for regular supplies to reach the inhabitants.

Inside the walls, houses and buildings were laid out in an orderly fashion. There were rows of rectangular houses made from mudbrick and stone. Each house featured the same spaces. There was a small entrance hall, a main living room, a few sleeping quarters, and a kitchen.

Most of the houses also had shrines carved in honor of local gods and protective deities. The inhabitants of Deir el-Medina typically worshiped Ptah (the patron deity of craftsmen), Amun (the chief deity of the entire Egyptian pantheon), Hathor (the goddess of the deceased, love, and the afterlife), and Meretseger (the cobra goddess of the necropolis).

Of course, the men in Deir el-Medina were not like the farmers found in agricultural villages that lined the banks of the Nile. Instead of working in the fields to feed the people of Egypt, they worked solely for the dead, focusing only on royal tombs. They were also employed by the state itself and paid in grain, beer, meat, and cloth. It is safe to conclude that Deir el-Medina was a closed society that functioned almost like a guild. This was where skills of tomb building were passed down from father to son.

As for the women of Deir el-Medina, they were far from passive figures despite not having to participate in the construction of the tombs. In fact, they enjoyed relatively elevated statuses compared to those living in other villages of Egypt. Since their husbands spent much of their time working at both the Valley of the Kings and Queens, women were the ones who managed the household. They also played a big role in the community's daily affairs. They were expected to oversee food preparation, weaving, and child-rearing, but they also had other responsibilities on their shoulders that went beyond just domestic duties. Those who married scribes or higher-ranking artisans were literate and involved in economic transactions. They sold goods and managed their property in their husbands' absence.

In contrast to women in many agricultural villages who toiled in the fields alongside their husbands, those in Deir el-Medina benefited from the regular wages their husbands received from the state. Through this financial stability, they were able to own property and inherit wealth. Some women even acted as petitioners before officials, seeking justice in disputes or addressing grievances related to household and inheritance issues.

The First Recorded Strike in History

However, not everything always went smoothly in Deir-el Medina. Believe it or not, this was the location where the first-ever strike occurred. Taking place sometime during the 12th century BCE, the workers of Deir el-Medina suddenly hung up their tools. Those in charge of carving the walls refused to even touch their chisels, and the painters let their paints dry, refusing to paint anymore until they received what was promised to them. It had been too long since they had received grains, and they knew the officials were aware of their discontent. When no action was taken, the workers left their secluded village and marched toward the mortuary temple of Ramesses III. There, they stood before the officials and administrators.

The sight of these workers undoubtedly stunned the officials. Never before had the craftsmen hung their tools for so long. It was their sacred duty to finish building the eternal homes of the pharaohs, so how could they leave the village? Luckily, this was not a violent rebellion. Not once did the workers attack the officials. Instead, they simply sat outside the temple, blocking its entrance so the officials could not complete their tasks. It was clear that they had no intention of leaving until their voices were heard.

The officials could not afford to spare any time. Those royal tombs had to be finished as soon as possible, so the officials scrambled to negotiate. Records suggest that instead of giving the workers their promised payment, they offered only excuses. The officials claimed that the grain had simply not arrived. However, the artisans were no fools. Even though they lived in an area far from the big cities, they were well aware of the state of the kingdom. They knew that the royal treasure was strained by wars and corruption. They knew that someone had mismanaged their rations. The workers refused to accept only words, so they moved from one temple to another, occupying spaces where the government could not ignore them.

Eventually, the authorities relented. They gave the workers what was promised to them. It was only after receiving their overdue wages that the workers returned home. Unfortunately, this was not the only time that the workers failed to get their payments.

Egypt faced yet another period of decline, as the kingdom's resources were stretched thin. The traditional wealth of the state, drawn from conquests and foreign tribute, was dwindling. Tomb robberies became increasingly common. Sadly, it was done not only by outsiders and criminals but also by the very individuals entrusted to guard the necropolis. Perhaps the saying is true: hard times call for desperate measures. As the years passed by, the once-reliable administration that oversaw tomb construction faltered, and payments to the artisans of Deir el-Medina became inconsistent. Delayed rations were the norm, resulting in frequent episodes where workers showed extreme discontent.

Things were getting worse for Egypt by the reign of Ramesses XI (r. 1107–1070 BCE). The kingdom was no longer the great power it had once been. With the emergence of the high priests of Amun in Thebes claiming power over the lands of Upper Egypt, the kingdom was officially fractured. War was constant in the lands, which further drained the state's coffers. With the royal treasure depleted, it was impossible for the kingdom to sustain the workforce at Deir el-Medina.

The village witnessed a gradual abandonment. Seeing no future ahead of them, families left the place they once called home. They either sought work elsewhere or blended into the growing power structures of Thebes. Some might have remained in the region, where they earned a living by working on less grand tomb projects. However, there were many others who managed to find employment with the temple priests. They had grown increasingly wealthy and influential ever since the kingdom fractured. Some people might have also chosen to migrate north, where they planned to build a new life in cities like Memphis or Tanis. Deir el-Medina finally transformed into a complete ghost town by 1070 BCE. Although the tombs that they had built remained, the majority of them were looted.

From here on, Egypt saw a major change in its burial traditions. Fewer royal tombs were commissioned, and if there were any, these tombs were built far simpler and less extravagant. Instead of massive hidden tombs in the cliffs, pharaohs of later periods, including those of the Third Intermediate Period and Late Period (1070–332 BCE), opted for large temple enclosures or burials in the Nile Delta region, where the power had shifted. Although temples continued to dot the vast lands, without the talent and dedication of the workforce at Deir el-Medina, their level of craftsmanship was never again fully replicated.

Deir el-Medina was eventually consumed by the relentless passage of time. For three thousand years, the once lively village lay forgotten beneath the desert sands. It was rediscovered in the 20th century by an Italian archaeologist named Ernesto Schiaparelli. Another set of excavations was carried out between 1922 and 1951. Headed by French Egyptologist Bernard Bruyère, a significant discovery was made during this dig. They unearthed not only artifacts but also the remains of an entire village, which was preserved in astonishing detail.

It was also in 1922 that the famous tomb of Tutankhamun was discovered by British archaeologist Howard Carter. Interestingly, the condition of the young pharaoh's tomb was almost unscathed. It remained intact and completely untouched by looters, unlike many other royal tombs in the Valley of the Kings. Tutankhamun's tomb was hidden beneath debris, which was likely the reason grave robbers had avoided it. Inside, the pharaoh's remains were accompanied by an array of treasures, from golden shrines to intricate chariots, jewelry, and, of course, the golden mask of Tutankhamun.

The interior of one of the chambers in Tutankhamun's tomb.[15]

Aside from the young pharaoh's tomb, the team of archaeologists also unearthed thousands of inscribed ostraca (pottery shards), which contained precious documents like personal letters, complaints, contracts, poems, and even satirical drawings. These findings shed greater light on the lives of the artisans who once lived in the forgotten village. Today, Deir el-Medina is considered one of the best-preserved archaeological sites in Egypt.

Chapter 5 – The Life of Senenmut: A Commoner Turned Royal Advisor

The heat was unrelenting, but the archaeologists were not planning on giving up just yet. For years, they had been excavating Hatshepsut's mortuary temple, brushing off every speck of dust that covered even the smallest inscription on the structure. The excavation and restoration works began in the early 20th century and lasted for nearly a century. It was first led by the Egyptian Antiquities Services until the mantle was passed to the Polish Academy of Sciences in the 1960s. The temple, with its elaborate designs, had suffered a lot over the millennia. However, each time the walls, columns, and statues were restored, a new story of the ancient Egyptians was unlocked, rewarding historians and scholars with more pieces of the puzzle.

The mortuary temple of Hatshepsut.[16]

One of the most intriguing discoveries was a series of statues. While it was completely normal for archaeologists to unearth statues with some of their parts chipped away or perhaps completely broken, these ones appeared rather peculiar. The statues were far from unscathed, but the culprit was neither time nor Mother Nature. Their faces were purposely chiseled off, and the inscriptions were deliberately erased. However, there was one particular statue that caught the attention of the archaeologists. One can only imagine the details of this life-sized figure back in its golden era, but when it was first unearthed by archaeologists, it was nothing more than a shadow of its former self. Although the name inscribed on its base had been erased, faint traces of the hieroglyphs could still be seen. Upon further examination, the archaeologists were able to read the name of the man: Senenmut. For someone who managed to get his own statue carved and placed in Hatshepsut's mortuary temple, Senenmut must have been an important figure who once walked alongside the Egyptian royals. But why was his statue purposely destroyed and its inscriptions chiseled off?

A stone with an inscription of Senenmut's name.[17]

The Obscured Early Life of Senenmut

Under the reign of Thutmose II, the Egyptian kingdom was balancing tradition and transition. Although the pharaoh's rule was quite short (he reigned for only thirteen years, compared to an average of fifteen to thirty years), Thutmose managed to maintain the centralized power of the monarchy. Minor rebellions and conflicts with its neighboring powers still occurred every once in a while, yet the kingdom was relatively at peace. Thebes also flourished during this period. As the spiritual and political heart of the kingdom, the city continued its role as a hub of religious devotion. Temples of Amun were constructed, with their obelisks reaching toward the sky.

Some might consider Senenmut's rise a story of rags to riches. He was thought to have built his life from the ground up, though scholars advise one to take this narrative with a grain of salt. After all, ancient Egyptian autobiographies, especially those authored by officials, were exaggerated and crafted to emphasize the values of loyalty, skills, and divine favor. Claiming that an individual rose from obscurity to a high rank was their way to highlight exceptional merit and curry favor with the gods and future benefactors.

Ancient writings about Senenmut, at least what is left of them, suggest Senenmut's origin was indeed humble. Born in a modest town near Thebes called Armant, he was the son of Ramose and Hatnofer. His parents had no titles. According to inscriptions uncovered in their tombs, Ramose was simply described as "revered," while Hatnofer was a "lady of the house." Scholars suggest that Ramose did not live long enough to see his son's career take off. Initially, he was buried simply, indicating that Senenmut had not yet obtained wealth from his career. Hatnofer died later on, and in contrast to Ramose, her burial, possibly arranged by Senenmut himself, was more lavish. Perhaps feeling obligated to improve his father's afterlife, Senenmut was said to have reburied Ramose alongside Hatnofer. Their tombs were then filled with the finest grave goods, perhaps in the hopes that his parents could have a comfortable life after death. Senenmut was not their only child. He had at least three brothers and two sisters, although none of them followed his footsteps to the Egyptian high office.

What exactly his earliest position was remains a mystery, but scholars speculate that Senenmut had a military background. This theory came from the paintings in his tomb, which depict Senenmut in a martial setting. However, without further evidence, it is unsure whether this depiction reflected his actual service or was merely symbolic. What we can be sure of is that his first major appointment came when Thutmose II rose to the throne. Senenmut was to serve the royal household. Then, at some point in time, Senenmut was made the tutor to Neferure, the daughter of Thutmose II and his wife, Hatshepsut.

A statue of Senenmut embracing Princess Neferure.[18]

It was an honor to be entrusted with the education and care of a royal child. This appointment showed the pharaoh trusted Senenmut. By constantly being at the side of the royal family, Senenmut began growing his influence. He was probably proud of his role since he frequently referenced his position as Neferure's tutor on his statues and inscriptions. One particular statue—now stored at the British Museum—showed the relationship that Senenmut had with the royal family. The statue depicted him cradling Neferure in a protective embrace, which was extraordinary, especially since the Egyptian royal family was seen as almost divine. Oftentimes, they were depicted standing far above the common people. It was already considered a privilege for a court official to be portrayed kissing the ground before a royal's feet, let alone a mere commoner embracing them in such an intimate manner.

Senenmut rose through the ranks again, reaching new heights after the kingdom witnessed the death of the pharaoh, Thutmose II. Although the late pharaoh left an heir when he departed to the Duat, his son (named Thutmose III) was only an infant. The power to govern Egypt was temporarily passed to Hatshepsut. It was common for an older female family member, especially mothers, to serve as regent until a young king came of age.

Despite Hatshepsut being in her late teens when she assumed the role, she was already ambitious. It was not entirely uncommon for a woman to act as regent, but Hatshepsut's approach was anything but typical. Aside from assisting in state matters until Thutmose III finally grew up, Hatshepsut began to absorb more and more power for herself. In contrast to other women in her position, she never remarried. This way, she could keep other powerful men from taking charge. Over time, Hatshepsut gained enough reputation and influence that she eventually managed to declare herself pharaoh.

This was a bold move. Hatshepsut was the second known female pharaoh, with the first being Sobekneferu, who ruled during the Middle Kingdom. She knew her reign would not be free from obstacles, especially when there were those who were not a fan of the idea that a woman had been placed on top of the hierarchy. In order to make her subjects see her as a legitimate ruler, Hatshepsut began wearing the Egyptian symbols of kingship. Her statues often depicted her wearing a false beard and the nemes headdress (the striped blue and gold crown-like cloth typically worn by male pharaohs).

A statue of Hatshepsut dressed in royal regalia typically worn by male rulers.[19]

Hatshepsut was a capable ruler. Her reign brought the kingdom stability and prosperity. With Egypt's immense wealth, the pharaoh was able to elevate the kingdom's cultural identity and influence. Monumental construction projects took place, and several trade expeditions, particularly to the rich land of Punt, were launched. The pharaoh excelled in her responsibilities with the help of her most trusted advisors, one of which was Senenmut.

Perhaps realizing Senenmut's loyalty and capabilities after observing him as a tutor to her daughter, Neferure, Hatshepsut thought it was high time to promote him to a higher position. Hatshepsut officially assumed the title of pharaoh during her seventh year as Thutmose's regent, and this was also when Senenmut was promoted to steward of Amun. In this new role of his, Senenmut was put in charge of the vast resources and wealth associated with the temple of Amun at Karnak. He was expected to manage the granaries, livestock, and every other resource that kept Egypt's economy alive.

Administration works were only the tip of the iceberg. Since he also held the title of overseer of works, Senenmut was also in charge of overseeing Hatshepsut's architectural projects across the kingdom, including the construction of two colossal obelisks at Aswan. Considered to be symbols of divine connection and political power, these obelisks stood at the gateway to the grand temple of Karnak. However, it was the mortuary temple of Deir el-Bahari (Hatshepsut's mortuary temple, also known as Djeser-Djeseru) that Senenmut was the proudest of.

The temple at Deir el-Bahari.[20]

To this day, this particular temple is considered one of the most remarkable architectural wonders of ancient Egypt. Constructed into the cliffs of Deir el-Bahri on the opposite side of the city Thebes (modern-day Luxor), the temple's main feature was its terraces, which rose in harmonious symmetry. The structure blended seamlessly with the natural backdrop. In every corner of the temple, one could set eyes on the many reliefs depicting Hatshepsut's reign, from her divine birth to a scene of her coronation to, of course, the famed expedition to Punt. When Hatshepsut launched the construction project of this temple, she was not only planning for it to become a funerary monument. It was also meant to stand as a statement of her legitimacy as a ruler, as well as her devotion to the god Amun.

Scholars agree that Senenmut played a role in the construction of Djeser-Djeseru, yet it is still uncertain whether or not he was the chief architect of the project. However, archaeologists found inscriptions of Senenmut with the title of "Overseer of Works of Amun at Djeser-Djeseru," suggesting that he must have played a crucial role in the construction at some point. There also exists another depiction of Senenmut that symbolizes his contribution to the construction of major buildings dated to this period. Currently housed at the Louvre Museum in Paris, this particular statue shows Senenmut holding a surveyor's rope.

Of course, this is not the only statue that was left behind; excavations have unearthed twenty-five in total. One of them shows Senenmut offering a sacred sistrum (a musical instrument used in religious rituals) to a god, while another depicts him holding a naos (a small shrine housing a statue of a god, typically located in the most sacred chamber of a temple). These depictions broke conventions since they portrayed a non-royal in poses commonly reserved for either the royals or the highest-ranking priests.

The most intriguing depiction of Senenmut was the one found at Hatshepsut's mortuary temple. Inscribed behind a doorjamb in the temple was Senenmut adoring the pharaoh. However, it was the inscription's hidden placement that brought speculation. Some question whether the addition of this inscription was ever approved by Hatshepsut herself, while there are also others who suggest that it symbolized an intimate bond between himself and the pharaoh.

His tombs also provide a little insight into his ambitions and personality. Interestingly, Senenmut commissioned at least two tombs for himself. One was located in Sheikh Abd el-Qurna (part of the Theban necropolis), while another could be found close to Hatshepsut's mortuary temple—the latter was unfinished for unknown reasons.

The entrance of Senenmut's underground tomb.[31]

His tombs, especially the one in Sheikh Abd el-Qurna, were far from modest since both were decorated lavishly with many inscriptions boasting his accomplishments. In ancient Egyptian tombs, it was common to have specific chambers or areas that were reserved for the gods. These chambers were usually where rituals were performed or offerings were left. Symbols of divine connection were also often displayed here. Senenmut had this special chamber built in his unfinished tomb. On its ceiling was a painting of a celestial diagram. While it could simply be viewed as a way to show respect to the gods, some saw it as his attempt to portray himself as someone extraordinary who did not only have a connection to the divine but also a deep knowledge of heavenly matters, such as astronomy.

Archaeologists have also unearthed his sarcophagus. What is interesting, though, is that it was fashioned using the same stone as contemporary royal sarcophagi. Even the decorations painted on it were almost identical to the styles used on those belonging to the royals. However, it was never finished, so scholars believe that it was highly unlikely that Senenmut was ever buried in it.

Senenmut and Hatshepsut as Lovers: Fact or a Rumor?

Gossip and rumors have always been a powerful tool in human societies, though it can work in two ways. It can help spread information, but at the same time, it can also cause harm. This tool existed even in ancient times. Gossip was a subtle killer; words could topple even the greatest figures of history.

The famous Greek philosopher Socrates, for instance, had carved his name as the most famous thinker of all time. Yet, he was never free from the dangers of rumors. Word spread, accusing him of corrupting the youth and dishonoring the gods. These rumors eventually led to his trial, where he was sentenced to death. Such tragedies show how rumors—no matter how small they started—could destroy even the most respected people. Whether it was done out of jealousy or fear or created by someone trying to gain power, it was—and still is—one of the most dangerous tools that can ruin lives.

The same thing possibly happened to Senenmut and Hatshepsut. As a commoner who successfully rose to extraordinary heights of influence, it is not surprising that his name became a favorite subject of speculation. Even though scholars suggest that their relationship was forged in trust and mutual ambition, rumors circulated in the royal court speaking of their intimate relationship. This rumor never died down, even after the two died. It survived for millennia and smeared their legacies.

Marriage was important in ancient Egypt. It was not only about forming familial bonds; it was also a way to keep Egyptian society and the economy stable. Men, especially those who held status and wealth, were expected to get married and have children. Therefore, it was highly unusual for Senenmut to remain a bachelor even after obtaining such influence in the kingdom. Combined with his close relationship with Hatshepsut, speculations were born, with the people wondering whether their relationship was indeed more than just being allies.

Although there is no definitive evidence that could confirm a romantic relationship between the two, scholars have found intriguing details that could serve as potential clues. Some suggest that their professional relationship was unusual. Senenmut was trusted by the queen so much that he was given an incredible amount of power and responsibility. Apart from roles where he oversaw various construction projects, Senenmut was also showered with many more titles and honors compared to other royal advisors before him. This subtly suggests that he was very important to Hatshepsut.

Other clues came from his imagery and inscriptions. It is impressive that Senenmut was allowed to create depictions of himself in a manner often reserved for royals. Not only did he have a statue of himself alongside Neferure, but the hidden carving showing himself honoring Hatshepsut was thought to hint at a closer, more private connection with the queen. There is also crude graffiti near the mortuary temple that depicts Hatshepsut with a man in inappropriate positions. The queen never remarried, and the only man close to her was Senenmut, so many believe the man in the graffiti is supposed to be Senenmut. There is no concrete evidence that it is him; while it is plausible that the graffiti reflects a real scandal, it is also highly likely that it was created in an attempt to damage her reputation as a female pharaoh.

It is well known that the ancient Egyptian society was deeply hierarchical. Any sort of breach in royal protocol would have been documented by critics, rivals, or enemies of the pharaoh. Thus, the lack of any explicit contemporary record of their relationship could prove that there was never a scandal to begin with. Furthermore, while women in ancient Egypt did have certain rights compared to other civilizations like the Greeks or the Romans, it was still difficult for a female pharaoh to navigate her reign all alone. Because of this, it made sense for Hatshepsut, who ruled in a male-dominated society, to rely on Senenmut's skills and loyalty. While it is clear that Hatshepsut's decision to not remarry after Thutmose II's death was so that she could avoid her power being diminished, Senenmut's decision to not marry until his death could simply indicate his dedication to his duties.

Senenmut in Later Years

Senenmut continued to be Hatshepsut's most trusted confidant throughout her rule. His career reached its zenith by the sixteenth year of the queen's reign. For a man of non-royal blood, it was beyond impressive that Senenmut was able to gain such authority. Yet, for unknown reasons, shortly after this time, records of his activities ceased abruptly, which signified his decline. Mysteriously, his tomb at Hatshepsut's mortuary temple was left unfinished. His statues and inscriptions faced vandalism, and they were purposely defaced and destroyed. However, what exactly did the royal advisor do for him to earn such a fate?

Of course, the first theory lies in his supposed relationship with Hatshepsut. If the rumors were true, it could very much be possible that their scandal stirred discontent among the court officials. After all, Senenmut had an ordinary background—he belonged neither to the noble nor had royal lineage. For a mere commoner to rise so quickly and earn a soft spot in the eyes of the queen might have led the court officials to turn against him. Another theory, though almost similar to the first one, simply suggests political jealousy. His skills and talent, along with his access to power, likely made him a target of envy among the elites. He had accumulated so many titles and honors. Although he earned them, some may view this as overreach. Egyptian court politics were also notoriously treacherous. Not everyone accepted Hatshepsut as their pharaoh, so it could be plausible that the officials plotted against Senenmut as part of their effort to weaken the queen's position.

Alternatively, Senenmut's sudden fall might have also been the result of Hatshepsut's own decisions. Perhaps she had grown weary of her trusted advisor, who had gained massive influence over her people. As a queen who had successfully navigated male-dominated power structures, Hatshepsut probably found it politically crucial to distance herself from Senenmut and eventually remove him from the court. Meanwhile, there are some historians who propose that Senenmut's decline was Thutmose III's doing. Now that he had come of age, Thutmose desired the throne and was not happy with Hatshepsut denying him his rights. He might have also seen Senenmut as an obstacle to his ascension, especially after witnessing the advisor's close relationship with the queen. Therefore, one of his first steps to reclaim his authority was to silence Senenmut and erase every trace of him.

He might have done this during the later years of Hatshepsut's reign when her power was visibly waning. Perhaps after obtaining the trust of certain factions within the court, Thutmose was able to eliminate Senenmut. With the queen's most powerful supporter gone, his way to the throne was confirmed. Whether it is true that Thutmose was the one responsible for Senenmut's fall remains debatable.

Scholars suspect that the pharaoh might have been the one who ordered the defacement of his statues and inscriptions. When Thutmose finally rose as pharaoh, he worked to erase Hatshepsut's legacy. Anything related to the former queen was destroyed. Since Senenmut was closely associated with her, the advisor also faced the same fate; his memory and evidence of his contributions were condemned to erasure.

Chapter 6 – The Lost Egyptian Labyrinth

Whenever the word "labyrinth" is mentioned, many may immediately conjure an image of the legendary maze in Greek mythology. That intricate structure was believed to have been designed by the Greek architect Daedalus to house the vicious half-man, half-bull known as the Minotaur. According to the ancient myth, King Minos of Crete commissioned the famed labyrinth after receiving the monstrous creature as a punishment from the Olympian gods. The king knew that killing the Minotaur outright would do nothing except invite even more wrath from the gods. The only solution to keep the creature away from mankind was to contain it in a prison so complex that none who entered, including the Minotaur itself, could find their way out. Daedalus succeeded in fulfilling the king's order. The Minotaur was doomed to remain in its prison until the creature eventually died at the hands of the hero Theseus.

The story of this labyrinth is nothing more than a myth. No concrete evidence has ever been unearthed that showed the existence of it. However, the same could not be said about Egypt. As the land of pyramids, sphinxes, and obelisks, it is not surprising that the kingdom also housed a grand labyrinth. Ancient historians claimed it was so colossal that it dwarfed even the grandest structures of its time. It was said to have stood near the shores of Lake Moeris in the region of Faiyum and left its visitors in complete awe, including the famed Greek historian of the ancient world, Herodotus.

The Father of History claimed to have seen the labyrinth with his own eyes during his travels across Egypt. Driven by knowledge and adventure, as well as tales of the past, Herodotus arrived in the Nile Delta sometime in the 5th century BCE. Having grown up in the Greek city of Halicarnassus when it was under the watchful eyes of the Persians, Egypt was a vastly different world from his own. Herodotus might have traveled southward along the Nile in the direction of the famed pyramids of Giza. He had, of course, heard of the magnificent structure, but he was not content with only words. When he finally arrived in Giza, the historian was left speechless. He traced the lines of the limestone blocks and wondered how many hands it had taken to shape such colossal tombs. He listened to priests narrating stories of the construction and the pharaohs who were interred in them. Herodotus took note of all this information, later compiling it in his books.

His next stop was the majestic temple of Amun at Karnak. Greece had intricate columns adorning its architectural wonders, yet the ones he witnessed at Karnak were on another level. The Egyptians constructed the pillars and adorned the walls with vibrant hieroglyphs and inscriptions as if the gods themselves would one day descend to the earth and reside in the temple. Here, Herodotus observed the priests performing their sacred rites and listened to tales of their mighty gods.

Herodotus also spent time in Memphis, where he learned more about the beliefs and religion of the ancient Egyptians. He heard about the sacred bulls of Apis and learned that crocodiles were considered sacred by some Egyptians, especially those who lived near Thebes and Lake Moeris. Each wonder he visited deepened his admiration for the kingdom. Despite describing the Egyptians as starkly different and rather peculiar compared to the Greeks, Herodotus held them in high esteem.

However, out of all the wonders that he had witnessed in the kingdom, none could rival the Labyrinth of Egypt. Some people today may imagine it as a maze, perhaps similar to the ones depicted in paintings or drawings of the famous Greek labyrinth. However, this labyrinth was far from the one told in the myth; the Labyrinth of Egypt did not consist of dark, twisting corridors. Rather, it was a sprawling two-story structure. It was so massive that it housed three thousand rooms. Herodotus told us that half of the rooms were above ground while another half was built beneath the earth. There were also twelve grand patios, built perfectly symmetrical. They were arranged in two rows of six, with each doorway facing its counterpart.

A depiction of the lost Labyrinth of Egypt.[38]

It took Herodotus only a single step into the labyrinth for his eyes to widen. The network of halls, chambers, and passageways before him seemed as if it was endless, stretching into eternity. The historian had Egyptian guides accompanying him. They permitted Herodotus to enter the upper rooms, which were all heavily adorned with elaborate carvings and reliefs. Some of them told stories of the many pharaohs who once ruled the kingdom. Others depicted their mighty gods and the performance of various sacred rites. Herodotus's eyes then darted to the stone ceilings above him and wondered how long it took the Egyptians to craft such intricate wonders. The courtyards were also meticulously designed. Constructed using white marble, each of the courtyards was encircled by a colonnade. The gap between these columns allowed natural light to shine through, giving the courtyard a sense of ethereal beauty.

Herodotus made his way through almost every part of the upper rooms. He walked along the colonnade courtyard, which connected to another intricate room, and then he passed through yet another courtyard, which connected to more rooms, halls, and galleries. Herodotus then noticed another section and was curious to explore the area. However, the Egyptian guides stopped him, claiming that he was forbidden from descending into the lower chambers. When asked why, the guides spoke in hushed tones. They told the historian that the lower chambers were reserved only for the tombs of the kings who built the labyrinth. Herodotus also learned that the underground chambers housed sacred rooms where the Egyptians kept their sacred crocodiles of the Nile. The historian could only imagine these chambers since he was not allowed to lay eyes on them.

A plan of the labyrinth by the 17ᵗʰ-century German Jesuit scholar Athanasius Kircher based on the descriptions provided by Herodotus.²⁴

Of course, Herodotus was not the only ancient writer to record and describe the labyrinth's splendor. Two centuries later, the Egyptian priest and historian of the 3ʳᵈ century BCE documented the architectural wonder. His writings, however, shed more light on the pharaohs who constructed it rather than details of the labyrinth itself. Another Greek historian, Diodorus Siculus, who built his reputation in 1st first century BCE, as well as the Greek geographer Strabo, also included colorful descriptions of the labyrinth. Strabo was one of the few who claimed to have seen the labyrinth with his own eyes. He was especially enthralled by the colossal scale of its courtyards and the seemingly endless chambers.

Word of this famed labyrinth even reached beyond the Aegean and into ancient Rome. Roman author Pliny the Elder left us with his writings, where he described the luxurious sense of the labyrinth's halls and its exquisitely carved stone pillars. The Roman geographer of the 1st century BCE, Pomponius Mela, also briefly mentioned the labyrinth in his writings, though his account was the least detailed compared to the others.

Interestingly, despite being written many years apart, these records contain a high degree of consistency. Each of them mentioned the twelve patios or courtyards, the thousands of chambers and their intricate designs, and the stone ceilings. Some even described a grand temple within the labyrinth that was encircled by forty marble columns. This remarkable consistency, spanning over six centuries from Herodotus to Pomponius Mela, suggests that the labyrinth indeed existed during their time.

The Purpose of the Labyrinth: Was it Ever Intended to Be a Maze?

The main reason behind the construction of this labyrinth has long perplexed scholars, especially when ancient writers provided different explanations in their books. While some suggested that it was initially commissioned as a palace for a ruler named Moteris, others claimed it was a tomb for a certain king named Moeris. There were also those who thought of the labyrinth as a grand temple to honor the sun. The Greek orator Aelius Aristides (117–181 CE), on the other hand, provided a whole different view. He dismissed the idea that the labyrinth had any practical function. Instead, he claimed that it was nothing more than a rhetorical symbol of Egypt's greatness. However, the labyrinth was believed to have been built many centuries before the orator was born, so it could be plausible that the structure had long succumbed to the test of time before Aristides came into the world.

Diodorus Siculus had his own theory regarding the purpose of the labyrinth. He suggested that it was built as a tomb for a certain Egyptian ruler who went by the name of either Mendes or Marrus. This does make sense, given how Egyptian pharaohs tended to construct elaborate burial structures for themselves. The only problem with this is that there are no known pharaohs under that name. Diodorus did not even provide a definitive timeline of Mendes's rule; he only mentioned that he rose many generations before the emergence of the legendary King Minos of Crete.

Some scholars believe that Diodorus might have mistaken Lake Moeris as the name of the ruler who constructed the labyrinth. This theory comes from the similarity between the name "Moeris" and the names "Mendes" or "Marrus." Since Herodotus specifically wrote about the labyrinth's location being near the lake, scholars suggest that there is a possibility that Diodorus misinterpreted the name of the lake as the king who built the wonder. Others argue that the ancient historian was not mistaken. They claim that the name Mendes could be a variation of an actual king who ruled the kingdom long ago. Archaeology professor Joseph MacGillivray, for instance, suggested that Mendes could be the same person as Amenemhat III, the sixth pharaoh of the Twelfth Dynasty.

Regardless of who exactly built the labyrinth, many argue that it would have been impossible for a structure of such scale to be built solely as a tomb. Ancient accounts wrote that it was once used as a political and religious center. Strabo described it as a gathering place for Egypt's regional governors and priests. According to the ancient writer, this was where the Egyptians held religious ceremonies, administrative meetings, and judicial proceedings. The layout of the labyrinth and its numerous chambers and courts lend credence to this theory. The labyrinth might have housed representatives from Egypt's many provinces or nomes. The underground chambers could have served as hidden sanctuaries where secret ceremonies took place.

Herodotus had a different view. In his writings, the historian stated that the twelve courts within the labyrinth were commissioned by the twelve kings who reigned over the kingdom jointly. Each of these courts was designated to a king, reflecting their collective rule. However, many scholars and historians are doubtful about this claim because there are no known historical records that could confirm a time when Egypt was ruled simultaneously by twelve kings. It is plausible that Herodotus mistakenly interpreted the inscriptions on the labyrinth; the twelve courts might have symbolized an administrative system rather than actual co-rulers.

Other scholars suggest that the labyrinth might have been a record-keeping center. If this theory is true, the many chambers in the labyrinth were probably where sacred scrolls and records of administrative, judicial, and economic affairs were stored. The countless passages might have been purposely designed to confuse people. Only those with authority knew the way, thus keeping the records perfectly safe.

Of course, there is also the idea that the labyrinth held a more symbolic meaning. The maze-like nature was probably designed to represent the order and chaos of the cosmos. This mirrored the Egyptian belief in the divine balance of the universe, Ma'at.

The Lost Location of the Labyrinth Unveiled

The labyrinth's exact purpose remains one of its two biggest mysteries, with the second being its location. Whether it was buried beneath the sands of Egypt, dismantled for its stone, or completely lost to the merciless passage of time, no one knows for sure. Ancient writers provided instructions or descriptions of its location, but they were rather vague. However, thanks to these clues, significant discoveries were finally made in the past few decades. The one made by William Flinders Petrie, for instance, shone a better light on the location of the labyrinth.

William Flinders Petrie is a familiar name, especially among Egyptologists, archaeologists, and scholars of the late 19th century. The British archaeologist was considered one of the pioneers of systematic archaeology in Egypt. He earned a reputation for his rigorous fieldwork and contributions that helped us understand the ancient Egyptian civilization. His biggest discovery was at Hawara. Here, Petrie uncovered a massive artificial stone plateau measuring at least three hundred meters by over two hundred meters. After more excavations and studies, Petrie eventually concluded that the stone foundation was the remnants of none other than the legendary labyrinth told by ancient historians.

This conclusion sparked interest, especially among the archaeological community. Some were doubtful that it had once been the site of the lost labyrinth, while others kept an open mind. The dimensions of the foundation, as well as its location close to the pyramid of Amenemhat II, suggest that it could have once supported the colossal labyrinth.

Some also presented the idea that the labyrinth itself was connected to Amenemhat's pyramid. It might have served a religious or funerary purpose. Following more excavations, Petrie later discovered that the structures around the pyramid were much larger and more complex than they previously thought, which led some scholars and historians to speculate that the labyrinth was far from a separate structure but rather a part of Amenemhat's grand construction plans.

The Middle Kingdom (c. 2055–1650 BCE), the period to which Amenemhat III belonged, was described by historians as a time when Egypt achieved political stability, tremendous economic growth, and a flourishing culture. The kingdom had endured the turmoil of the First Intermediate Period, during which time two dynasties vied for power. It was not until the rise of Mentuhotep II of the Eleventh Dynasty that the Egyptians were finally able to rediscover a glimmer of hope for their kingdom. The people saw the expansion of administrative reforms, extensive trade networks, and the start of more impressive architectural projects. While it was typical for pharaohs to cement their reputation through military campaigns, the rulers of the Middle Kingdom were also eager to solidify their legacy through grand construction programs. Pyramids continued to fill the kingdom's map, along with majestic temples and vast mortuary complexes.

Egypt witnessed an even greater period of prosperity and expansion when the throne was passed to Amenemhat III. Reigning over the Nile for nearly forty-five years, his name is often remembered as one of the most famous builders of ancient Egypt. The Faiyum region (also spelled as Fayoum), in particular, experienced rapid upgrades, eventually transforming into a key agricultural and administrative hub. This was largely due to its irrigation improvements and close proximity to Lake Moeris. Perhaps seeing the strategic importance of the region, Amenemhat later chose it as the site for his resting place.

This region was not his first choice, though. The pharaoh had already commissioned the construction of his pyramid at Dahshur. Now famously known as the Black Pyramid, its initial construction was full of structural flaws. It suffered from foundational instability. Cracks were said to have constantly appeared within its corridors and chambers, which made it impossible to house the remains of the pharaoh once the time came. By the fifteenth year of his reign, Amenemhat III had shifted his focus from Dahshur to Hawara, which was a short distance away from the center of Faiyum and Lake Moeris.

The Black Pyramid at Dahshur was not entirely abandoned. Instead of becoming the eternal resting place for the pharaoh, it was repurposed as a burial site reserved for several royal women, especially those who had blood relations to Amenemhat himself. The pharaoh was later interred at Hawara. Unlike the pyramid at Dahshur, his tomb in Hawara featured a more stable design and improved structural integrity.

Approximately twelve kilometers south of his pyramid, archaeologists unearthed another significant structure: the tomb of his daughter, Neferuptah. This adds more weight to the argument that Hawara was an elaborate mortuary complex serving multiple purposes beyond being the eternal home of Amenemhat III alone. Based on the sheer scale of the labyrinth as described by the ancient writers, some scholars proposed that the structure was possibly an essential part of this funerary site.

Many may wonder how the labyrinth disappeared completely despite its colossal size and complex design. Flinders Petrie answered this query by explaining the possibility of the labyrinth being dismantled and its stones reused for other purposes. This theory revolves around Ptolemy II when Egypt was in its Hellenistic period. Scholars suggested that the pharaoh might have used much of the labyrinth's stone to construct the nearby town of Shedet, better known as Crocodilopolis (it was built to honor Ptolemy's wife, Arsinoe). However, the total destruction of such a monumental structure remains a hot subject of debate. Some argue that the dismantling of the labyrinth alone was not enough for the structure to disappear completely; these scholars suggest that natural factors also contributed to its disappearance. The shifting river patterns in the Faiyum regions could have played a role too. Looting might have occurred over the centuries. The only thing left for us today is its stone base.

Another Clue

Although many accepted the conclusion made by Petrie, which suggested the enormous stone slab was the foundation of the long-lost labyrinth, there were those who were not entirely convinced. The most prominent individual to challenge this conclusion was a Belgian researcher named Louis de Cordier.

Cordier revisited Petrie's finding of the enormous stone platform. According to the ancient descriptions written by Herodotus and others, they spoke of a grand structure with an imposing stone ceiling. The roof was so massive that it covered the entire complex beneath it. The mention of this stone ceiling was repeatedly mentioned in multiple sources; one documented how the ceiling seemed like an unbroken stretch of stone, while another highlighted how the entire roof was made of a single solid slab. If these descriptions were true, then what Petrie thought was a foundation could actually be the labyrinth's roof. This means the rest of the structure was never dismantled or lost; rather, it was hidden beneath the earth.

This possibility changed everything. However, Cordier knew that excavating the site would not be easy. Traditional digging methods were definitely out of the question because the massive stone layer was not ordinary rubble or sand but rather a solid—or perhaps artificial, if it were really the roof of the labyrinth—plateau. Any attempt to break through it would cause irreparable damage to the rest of the structure. Furthermore, the labyrinth was believed to have an extensive network of chambers and near-endless passageways. An uncontrolled excavation could negatively impact the delicate architectural features. To avoid these big risks, Cordier and his team chose a non-invasive method: ground penetrating radar.

Known as the Mataha Expedition, Cordier and his team finally received good news after years of planning. In February 2008, the Supreme Council of Antiquities of Egypt granted permission for Cordier to conduct a full-scale geophysical survey on the same site where Petrie had previously explored. Hoping that the mystery of the labyrinth could be uncovered, Cordier brought in a team of specialists from the National Research Institute of Astronomy and Geophysics (NRIAG) to join the mission. Equipped with state-of-the-art radar equipment, their main objective was to scan the site, specifically beneath the stone plateau, without disturbing it.

Anticipation ran high. The team was hoping for even the smallest sign that there were structures hidden below. When positive results came in, Cordier was pleased. It turned out that the radar had detected a massive structure buried beneath the surface, with the depths ranging from eight to twelve meters. What was even more astonishing was that the scans also showed a precise grid pattern, which could possibly be an arrangement of chambers and thick walls, forming an extensive, well-organized complex. The team then discovered that these structures exhibited high resistivity, which meant that there was a presence of stone or possibly granite. This was an astounding discovery since they perfectly matched the ancient descriptions. At this point in time, the world was confident that this physical evidence confirmed the existence of the famed labyrinth.

These positive results were published in the scientific journal of the NRIAG in the fall of 2008. Their discoveries were widely shared at a public lecture at Ghent University in Belgium, which was attended by dozens of scholars and historians. Members of the press were also present since the announcement had sent ripples throughout the archaeological community. This could very well be one of the most significant discoveries of ancient Egypt's grandest wonder.

Unfortunately, hopes were crushed when everything suddenly fell silent. Without warning, the Supreme Council of Antiquities of Egypt imposed an unexpected restriction. Not only were all discussions about the labyrinth halted, but any communication about the findings was also suddenly prohibited. The authorities gave only one reason: Egyptian national security sanctions. Disappointed, some dismissed the result without questions, yet many others, including Cordier himself, thought the decision was strange and unexpected. A few questions linger to this day. Why would such an important historical discovery be suppressed? What was so dangerous about revealing the truth behind the labyrinth?

Cordier waited for two more years, holding on to what was left of his hope. However, by June 2010, it was clear that further examinations would not happen. The mystery would remain unsolved. The labyrinth was left buried not only beneath the sands but also beneath the layers of bureaucratic silence.

Despite the silence, Cordier's expedition breathed new life into the mystery that had puzzled many for centuries. More theories arose from the unanswered questions. While some suggested that the Egyptian government was actually concerned about this renewed attention, fearing that the site might face destruction or even looting, others believe there was a more paranormal reason.

Ancient Egypt has long been associated with curses, especially those involving tombs and sacred sites. The most famous of these is the curse of Tutankhamun's tomb. This curse has already been debunked, yet there are still some who believe in the supernatural consequences of messing with Egyptian tombs. Some speculate the same about the labyrinth; they believe the site also holds a curse.

Regardless of the reason, we can at least be assured that the Labyrinth of Egypt was not just a legend or tale created by ancient writers. It is currently buried beneath the desert, waiting to be unearthed one day.

Chapter 7 – The Nubian Pharaohs: Egypt's Forgotten Dynasty

The Egyptians could do nothing but witness their kingdom slowly descend into a period of weakness, division, and chaos. The last time they had ever seen a capable ruler on the throne was when Ramesses III wore the double crown. Egypt was already in turmoil when the Sea Peoples launched their campaigns, yet the pharaoh succeeded in repelling the invaders. However, his victories came at a heavy cost. The Egyptian treasury, which once had gold flowing like the Nile itself, was now nearly empty following years of conquests and war. Corruption began to seep into the royal court, and the military gradually shrank in both strength and effectiveness.

Then, sometime in 1170 BCE, came the strike at Deir el-Medina. However, this was not the only chaos that Egypt had to endure. By the time Ramesses III was assassinated, Egypt continued to spiral into a state of decline. His successors were weak rulers who failed to hold the empire together. Not only did the kingdom's wealth deteriorate, but Egypt also lost control of a few of its prized territories, such as Canaan and Nubia. It was clear that the kingdom was fracturing.

Soon, another power began to rise that challenged the authority of the pharaoh. For years, Amun had been one of the kingdom's most important deities. Lands and riches were typically granted to the priests of Amun by past rulers, allowing them to grow incredibly wealthy. By the Twentieth Dynasty, the temple of Amun in Karnak was essentially a state within a state. Not only did the temple control the lands, but its priests were also in charge of thousands of workers.

During this time, Egypt was under the rule of Ramesses XI, the last ruler of the Twentieth Dynasty. Despite the pharaoh still sitting on top of the hierarchy, a certain individual suddenly declared himself the ruler of Upper Egypt. His name was Herihor, the high priest of Amun in Thebes. With Ramesses XI's power reduced only to the north and the priests of Amun controlling Upper Egypt (located in the south), the kingdom was officially divided into two. Gone were the times when pharaohs were seen as the almighty ruler, second only to the gods.

The Arrival of the Libyans

Egypt was now vulnerable, especially to ambitious foreigners who wished to claim the land. The Libyans, for instance, held such an ambition. The Libyans did not always see eye to eye with the Egyptians. They once fought against the kingdom until the era of the New Kingdom when pharaohs began hiring them as mercenaries. In return for loyal service, they were granted land and opportunities, allowing them to rise through the ranks. Some earned enough trust from the pharaohs and even became powerful local rulers. Eventually, the Libyans grew so bold that they believed they no longer needed the pharaoh at all.

This could be seen in 945 BCE when a certain Libyan chieftain known as Shoshenq I declared himself the new pharaoh of Egypt. His rule started the Twenty-second Dynasty, marking the first time a foreigner rose to power from within Egypt's own system—unlike the Hyksos kings of the Fifteenth Dynasty, who had taken control through conquest. The pharaohs of this new dynasty ruled from Tanis, a city in the Eastern Delta. They never succeeded in claiming full control over the kingdom since the authority in Upper Egypt belonged to the priests of Amun. The priests refused to acknowledge these Libyan kings as the true rulers of Egypt, which led to the further fragmentation of the kingdom. Many more individuals, often chieftains of the other small territories, soon claimed their right to the throne, worsening the already weakening kingdom.

By the time of the Twenty-third Dynasty (c. 818–730 BCE), Egypt was nearly drowning. There were as many as four or perhaps five different individuals who claimed to be the rightful pharaoh of the kingdom.

Tefnakht Challenged the Priests of Amun

Tefnakht was another powerful individual who sought to see Egypt united again—but of course, it would be under his rule. In order to challenge the Theban priests controlling Upper Egypt, the warlord knew he had to muster every force he could on the Nile Delta. Luckily, Tefnakht was a skilled strategist. Even though he achieved little to no direct conquests, the ruler from Sais succeeded in forging alliances with other rulers of the Delta. With his power and reputation growing each day, Tefnakht began to turn his attention southward. He marched his forces to Middle Egypt and captured the cities that dotted the region.

His advance undoubtedly alerted the priests of Amun. If he were to succeed in entering Thebes, the last stronghold of the priests, Tefnakht would achieve his goal. Once he obtained total domination of both Lower and Middle Egypt, the warlord would be granted a clear pathway to Upper Egypt and even Nubia. The priests of Amun knew they could not rely solely on themselves to defeat the advancing warlord, so they chose to reach for outside help. They turned to Piye, the Nubian king of Kush.

The Rise of the Kushite Kingdom

As early as the Middle Kingdom, the Egyptians valued Nubia. It was thought to be a land of immense wealth. To keep a close eye on the region, the Egyptians began building forts in the area, installing garrisons and trading posts along the Nile in the hopes they could get their hands on the region's resources. When the New Kingdom began, the Nubians began to lose their authority. Pharaohs of the era, particularly Thutmose I and Thutmose III, poured extensive amounts of money to push into the Nubian lands. Eventually, the region was under the complete control of the Egyptians. From there on, Egyptian temples began to fill the region, and their religious practices were imposed on the locals. Nubian rulers, referred to as the viceroys of Kush, were appointed as representatives of the pharaohs.

For centuries, Nubia, also known as Kush, became an extension of the Nile kingdom. The Kushites adopted Egyptian customs and even worshiped the same gods as the Egyptians, particularly Amun. Their arts were also influenced by the Egyptians, as well as their government structure. However, Egypt was not meant to rule over Kush for too long.

When Egypt went into decline by the time of the Third Intermediate Period (c. 1070-664 BCE), its control over Kush had greatly weakened.

Seeing an opportunity to break free from the once-mighty kingdom, the Kushites claimed their independence sometime around 1000 BCE. Gone were the days when the viceroys of Kush had to report to the Egyptian pharaohs. Napata, a city near the sacred mountain of Gebel Barkal, was made the beating heart of this blossoming kingdom. Now known as the Kingdom of Kush, it soon turned into a powerful force in the south.

The sacred mountain Gebel Barkal, believed to be the residence of the god Amun.[16]

Regardless of being free from the grasp of the Egyptians, the Kushites still embraced the Egyptian culture. Amun was still greatly worshiped, with temples dedicated to the god constructed in a blend of both Egyptian and Nubian styles. As their influence expanded, the Kushites managed to gain control over the lands that were once under Egypt's control. With these newly obtained territories, the rulers of Kush grew wealthier. With more power in their hands, they grew more ambitious. As a result, the Kushites began to turn their gaze north toward Egypt.

The relationship between these two kingdoms was not always hostile. In fact, the Kushites still maintained close ties with the priests of Amun in Thebes; after all, they shared the reverence of the same god. In many ways, Kush and Upper Egypt became natural allies. They were united in their devotion to Amun, while the rest of Egypt remained divided among warlords and foreign rulers. So, when the priests sent a plea for aid, the reigning Kushite king at the time, Piye, did not hesitate to answer with reinforcements.

Piye rose to the throne in the 8th century BCE. A devout follower of Amun, the Kushite king viewed the fragmentation of Egypt as a violation of divine will. He saw the warlords who had claimed control over Egypt not as legitimate rulers but rather as greedy usurpers who had strayed far from the path of Ma'at. Piye thought it was his sole duty to restore Egypt. With an army of hardened Kushite warriors, exceptionally skilled archers, and his Egyptian allies, who were loyal to the Theban priests, Piye launched his campaign. He marched northward to Upper Egypt.

Thebes was pleased with the arrival of Piye and his forces. He was thought to be its savior. The Thebans welcomed the Kushite king and escorted him to the temple of Amun at Karnak. Here, he was believed to have prayed and made offerings to the god. The priests of Amun then proclaimed him the rightful ruler of Egypt. With the blessings of the gods and the priests, Piye set forth on his divine mission to reunite the vast kingdom. He marched toward the cities of Middle Egypt. Some surrendered willingly after seeing the king was a savior sent by Amun, while others attempted to resist. However, none could rival the might of the Kushite forces. The warlords of Middle Egypt, who had once ruled as independent rulers, eventually bowed down to the Kushite king. Some even sent him gifts, hoping they could get on Piye's good side. The king was not interested in bribes, though; he wanted only their loyalty.

At Sais, Tefnakht was growing wary. He heard news of Piye's advance and the king's success in gaining control of many territories. The warlord quickly formed a coalition of Delta rulers to go against the Kushite king. Among them were Osorkon IV of Tanis, a ruler whose background could be traced back to the Libyan dynasties. Others were powerful rulers from Herakleopolis and Memphis. They were hopeful that, together, they could stop Piye from snatching their crowns.

Nevertheless, their nightmare came true. Piye laid a siege on Herakleopolis. It was considered one of the most important strongholds on the path to Lower Egypt. The exact duration of the siege remains unknown, but according to Piye's victory stela, it was swift. When the city's defenses finally crumbled, its ruler, Peftjauawybast, was left with no other choice but to surrender. This, however, was only the beginning.

Following this victory, Piye advanced to the seat of power for Lower Egypt, Memphis. It was crucial for Piye to repeat his success here since Memphis was the stronghold of Tefnakht's coalition. Having the city under his control meant he could easily break the rest of his enemies.

Memphis was well defended; fortified walls protected its subjects at all sides, and the Nile was a natural barrier. The defenders showed their loyalty to Tefnakht by fighting fiercely against the Kushites. Yet, as their resources dwindled, it was only a matter of time before they eventually lost hope and succumbed to their fate. Piye's army, on the other hand, was relentless; the king himself was said to have ordered his men to fight as if there were no tomorrow. The Kushite forces attacked from the river, overwhelming Tefnakht's army. Memphis fell after a few days of intense battle. This victory led the other leaders of the Delta coalition to surrender to Piye.

Tefnakht was hit with the realization that he had lost. However, he refused to face Piye directly. Instead, the warlord fled northward, hoping he could remain safe behind the walls of his capital city, Sais. Piye had all the might and resources to pursue Tefnakht, yet he chose not to. His mission was to restore order, not cause destruction. His key allies had already surrendered and sworn loyalty to the Kushite king. Tefnakht eventually sent messengers to Piye, acknowledging his supreme rule over Egypt. The warlord never appeared before the new pharaoh of Egypt.

With the two lands of Egypt now reunited, Piye's divine task was accomplished. Interestingly, Piye did not remain in Egypt. He never forgot his background; Piye was a Kushite, not Egyptian, king. After vanquishing his enemies and consolidating his power, Piye planned to journey back to his kingdom. He was said to have visited the great temples of Egypt before his departure, where he spent time performing rituals before the great gods. This was to reaffirm his divine right to rule. Then, the new pharaoh of Egypt left, making his way south to the capital of Kush, Napata.

Although Piye was an absent ruler (he ruled from his homeland), Egypt was able to taste a pinch of peace once again. Before leaving, Piye made sure he left a system of governance that ensured stability. Egyptian officials were given a certain degree of autonomy, and the majestic temples in Egypt continued to flourish. Religious traditions, especially those done in honor of Amun, were also revitalized.

Piye's Death, Taharqa's Rise, and the Might of the Assyrians

In contrast to other kings and rulers who often met their fate either on the battlefield or through assassinations, Piye left the world rather peacefully. He died in his homeland of Kush. His remains were buried in a manner similar to the Egyptian tradition. His pyramid, though modest in size compared to the grand pyramids of Giza, can be found in El-Kurru, near Napata.

El-Kurru, located to the south of Jebel Barkal.[26]

Despite his death, Egypt did not immediately descend into another episode of chaos. The Kushite throne was passed to Piye's brother, Shabaka, who was also given the double crown of Egypt. Few sources were left that can lead us through the journey of Shabaka's life, but we do know that the king strengthened the Kushite rule over Egypt. There were no major conflicts that took place during his reign, but another misfortune was brewing. This time, it would come from the east.

During Shabaka's reign, a certain figure was building his reputation. Known as Taharqa, he was the son of the great Piye himself; however, some sources claim that he was actually his nephew. Being raised in the royal court of Napata, it is not a surprise that Taharqa grew up to be an ambitious royal. Sources suggest that Taharqa began his career serving as a military commander, gaining precious experience in warfare. Having spent much of his early life in Egypt, the Kushite prince was well versed in state matters.

Since religious devotion was placed above all else, especially when his name would be on the list of rulers of Kush, it was of the utmost importance that Taharqa commit himself to the spiritual world. He was said to have constantly traveled to Thebes when he was a young man, forming strong ties with the priesthood of Amun.

However, since succession in Kush was based on seniority, Taharqa was not the next in line when Shabaka passed away. Instead, the throne was passed to Shebitku. His relation to both Piye and Shabaka is unclear; some suggest he was either Shabaka's nephew or younger brother. Like his predecessors, Shebitku maintained control over Egypt, continuing the policies of the previous Kushite kings. This was also the time of the greatest test the dynasty faced: the Assyrian Empire.

The Assyrians first rose to power around the 14th century BCE, with their roots tracing back to northern Mesopotamia (modern-day Iraq), but it was not until the 9th century BCE that the empire began to transform into one of the dominant forces of the ancient world. For years, they relentlessly expanded their influence across the Near East, eventually becoming an empire that could rival both Egypt and Kush. The Assyrians were known to be militaristic people. Apart from being famed for their iron weapons, the Assyrians were also exceptionally skilled in siege warfare. Over the years, they successfully conquered a collection of territories from Babylonia to the Levant.

Tensions between Assyria and Egypt became apparent when the Assyrians were under the reign of Sargon II (722-705 BCE). It began when Egypt, which was under the rule of Shabaka, clearly showed support for the anti-Assyrian rebellions that erupted in kingdoms like Judah and Philistia. Even though Sargon managed to quell these rebellions, resistance remained in the Levant, with Egypt continuously supporting them.

Taharqa finally inherited the throne following the passing of Shebitku in 690 BCE. His early reign saw a flourishing of Egyptian culture and military power. He undertook massive building projects, restoring temples and monuments across the land. However, at the same time, the conflict between Assyria and Egypt had already escalated. The Assyrians did not only see Egypt as a distant influence that meddled in Levantine affairs but also as a direct enemy. The Assyrian king was well aware of the land's rich resources and history. However, to get his hands on the land, they first needed to go against the Kushite rulers.

In 674 BCE, the Assyrians, under King Esarhaddon, marched into Egypt. This marked the beginning of their invasion of the kingdom. With his massive army, Esarhaddon trampled through the Levant, crushing anyone who dared to stand in his path. He had a clear goal: break Kushite rule over Egypt and claim the double crown for himself. The mission was far from a piece of cake, though, as Taharqa was not an easy opponent. With haste, the Kushite pharaoh mustered his forces, gathering soldiers who hailed from both Egypt and Nubia.

The two forces eventually clashed. Neither the exact date nor location was ever confirmed due to the lack of records, but Taharqa successfully repelled the Assyrian invasion. This was a major victory for the Egyptians and a humiliation for the Assyrian war machine. Nevertheless, Assyria was not a kingdom that knew how to back down.

Esarhaddon, perhaps fueled by rage, launched a second, much larger invasion in 671 BCE. The preparations were meticulous since the king could not bear to face yet another episode of humiliation. Esarhaddon made sure to use his superior siege tactics to break the fortified walls of Egypt. With his massive army—his numbers were even bigger this time around—the Assyrians overwhelmed the Egyptian defenses. Although Taharqa himself fought bravely, the odds were clearly against him. Memphis, the great city of Lower Egypt, crumbled and fell to the Assyrians. Esarhaddon then pushed south. Taharqa slowly realized there was no easy way out, and he retreated to Upper Egypt and eventually back to Kush.

Again, Egypt witnessed a change of hands in the royal court. This was the beginning of the end of the Kushite rule of Egypt. Esarhaddon installed puppet rulers in the north, which allowed the Assyrians to gain firm control over Lower Egypt. Taharqa attempted to reassert his dominance over the Nile Valley, but the Assyrians were too powerful. It was clear that Egypt was too far out of his reach.

Tantamani, the Last Pharaoh of the Nubian Dynasty

Unless divine intervention happened, it was impossible for the Kushites to reclaim their foothold in Egypt. Following the loss of Lower Egypt to the Assyrians, Taharqa spent the remainder of his life in Napata. He ruled over the Kingdom of Kush and remained a powerful figure in the region. The Kushite king passed away in 664 BCE, possibly due to natural causes. His remains were buried in the royal necropolis of Nuri.

The throne was then passed to his successor, Tantamani. He was either the son or nephew of Taharqa. Tantamani was not planning on sitting still while the Assyrians had their claws in Lower Egypt. During this time, the Assyrians had Necho I acting as their puppet ruler in Lower Egypt.

Tantamani refused to accept the loss of Egypt and soon declared his divine right to rule both Kush and Egypt. Just as Piye before him, Tantamani also believed that the gods had chosen him to restore Ma'at. He believed that balance and order had been disrupted when Egypt was put under Assyrian rule. Sometime in 663 BCE, Tantamani launched his campaign to retake the kingdom of the Nile. He first had his eyes on Thebes, which had long been a stronghold of Kushite influence. Since the priests of Amun were loyal to the Nubian dynasty, Tantamani was warmly welcomed as the kingdom's rightful ruler.

In Thebes, Tantamani began working on the preparation of his campaign. In order to push north, he had to gather a force; he did so by mustering an army of Kushite warriors and Egyptian supporters. His goal was straightforward: retake Memphis, drive out the Assyrians, and restore Kushite dominance over Egypt. His campaign went well in the beginning. As his forces advanced, many cities fell to his army. Puppet rulers who had been installed by the Assyrians fled for their lives. Even Necho I of Lower Egypt was incapable of stopping the wrath of the Kushite king. Eventually, Tantamani's next target was none other than Memphis, the very city that had fallen to the Assyrians years prior.

Tantamani's Temporary Victory

As soon as he reached Memphis, Tantamani did not hesitate to launch a full-scale assault on the city. His warriors stormed the fortified walls and obliterated those who stood in their way. Fierce and brutal fighting ensued. Necho I was among those who lay lifeless on the ground. Tantamani succeeded in recapturing Memphis, and with this victory, it was not a surprise that other remaining Egyptian warlords came running to submit to his rule.

The Kushite king achieved what his predecessor had failed to accomplish. He had successfully reclaimed Egypt's heartland and drove out the Assyrian-backed rulers. For a brief moment, it seemed as if Amun was on their side. However, this was nothing more than just a temporary victory.

News of Tantamani's success soon reached the ears of the reigning king of Assyria, Ashurbanipal. He was furious and saw the Kushites' campaign as an act of defiance. He refused to see any other outcome; Ashurbanipal wanted Tantamani and the Kushites crushed. In 663 BCE, the Assyrian king wasted no time in launching another massive invasion of Egypt. This time around, the Assyrians refrained from showing even the smallest glint of mercy. They were determined to destroy Kushite rule once and for all.

Along with siege engines and battle-hardened mercenaries obtained from the Levant, the Assyrians marched into Egypt with terrifying speed. It did not take long for them to recapture Memphis. Tantamani's forces, though they fought valiantly, were forced to retreat to Thebes. However, the Assyrians, perhaps driven by their rage, did not sheathe their weapons just yet. They marched to Thebes, and for the first time in history, Egypt's religious capital was completely sacked. Ancient historians recorded the Assyrians' act of plundering the great temples of Amun. They took away the sacred relics and treasure, bringing them back to their capital, Nineveh. Thebes was left in ruins.

Tantamani was forced to leave the Nile kingdom and return to Nubia. Despite continuing to rule his kingdom from Napata, he never set foot on Egyptian soil again. With both Thebes and Memphis securely under Assyrian control, Ashurbanipal's goal was achieved: Kushite rule in Egypt had been wiped out.

To secure their power in Lower Egypt, the Assyrians installed Psamtik I as their new puppet ruler. This, however, was a mistake, as Psamtik I was different from the previous puppet kings. He succeeded in establishing full independence from the Assyrians. Psamtik was the founder of the Twenty-sixth Dynasty, the last great Egyptian dynasty before the Persian conquest. The age of the Kushite pharaohs had come to an end, but with Psamtik I on the throne, the Egyptians could live under the rule of a native pharaoh once more.

Chapter 8 – The Sacred Lake of Karnak

Hatshepsut passed away sometime in 1458 BCE, possibly due to natural causes. The queen reigned for over twenty years, making her one of the longest-reigning and most successful female pharaohs in Egyptian history. Of course, her passing paved the way for Thutmose III to finally claim the crown. The pharaoh inherited a kingdom that was already at its height. Nevertheless, Thutmose never thought of laying low; the pharaoh wished to expand Egypt further and build a reputation for himself that could rival his predecessors.

Also known as the "Napoleon of Egypt" (the term was given by the American Egyptologist James Breasted), the pharaoh was best known for his military campaigns, especially those he launched in the Levant. Through this series of campaigns, Egypt was able to expand its territory, eventually establishing it as a dominant power in the ancient Near East. It was also through these successful conquests that Egypt gained more wealth. Apart from tributes, the kingdom also gained access to valuable resources, including cedar from Lebanon and precious metals from the Sinai Peninsula.

It is safe to say that Thutmose was a good ruler. Not only did he excel on the battlefield, but the pharaoh was also a builder. He was well aware that Egypt's spiritual and cultural identity was intertwined with its religious institutions, particularly the worship of Amun. Thutmose himself was a devout follower of Amun, so it is not surprising that the pharaoh sought any way to glorify the god. Also, in an effort to consolidate his own divine kingship, Thutmose launched dozens of construction projects throughout the years of his reign (he ruled for over fifty years). After all, Egypt had amassed a substantial amount of wealth from its successful military campaigns. Among his many contributions to the architecture of Egypt, the one that stood out the most was his work on the Karnak Temple Complex.

The Karnak Complex

The Karnak Temple Complex was already over five centuries old when Thutmose III came to the throne. Its origins could be traced back to the Middle Kingdom when Pharaoh Senusret I of the Twelfth Dynasty established the site as a sanctuary to honor the chief deity, Amun. The complex was initially filled with modest structures, but it evolved into an impressive site as time went on. Thutmose I,

Hatshepsut, and Amenhotep were a few of the pharaohs who contributed to Karnak's expansion. However, it was under Thutmose III that the complex underwent significant enhancements. It was later transformed into a crucial site that symbolized the divine connection between the gods and the pharaohs.

Karnak was situated on the east bank of the Nile in Thebes (modern-day Luxor). Considered today as one of the largest religious sites ever constructed, this two-hundred-acre sanctuary was built as a dedication to the king of the Egyptian gods, Amun, and his consort Mut and their son Khonsu.

Carved columns at the Hypostyle Hall of Karnak.[38]

Some might agree that one of the most impressive features of Karnak is the Hypostyle Hall, which is described as a forest of columns. There are 134 intricately carved columns in total, with some reaching over 20 meters. These columns were arranged in sixteen rows and adorned with various hieroglyphs and depictions of the pharaohs honoring the gods. The Karnak Temple Complex was also the home to the famed ceremonial pathway known as the Avenue of Sphinxes. Flanked by rows of ram-headed sphinxes, this pathway connected Karnak to the Luxor Temple and played a major role in religious rituals.

Ram-headed sphinxes lined up along the Avenue of Sphinxes.[39]

Perhaps one of the most notable expansion projects commissioned by Thutmose III was the Akhmenu. Also known as the Festival Hall, this structure could be located in the eastern precinct of the temple complex. It was designed specifically for the Heb-Sed festival, which was a royal jubilee that celebrated the renewal of the pharaoh's power. Besides exquisite carved reliefs that told stories of Thutmose's military successes and offerings to Amun, the Akhmenu also featured a botanical garden. This, however, was not a real garden but a stone-carved relief that depicted exotic plants and animals like giraffes and ibexes brought back from Thutmose's military campaigns in Syria and Nubia.

Akhmenu or the Festival Hall of Thutmose III.[80]

Thutmose III added a few obelisks at Karnak. These towering structures, often gilded to reflect the sunlight, were built in honor of Amun and the sun god, Ra. The pharaoh also played a hand in expanding the temple's boundaries. He added the sixth pylon, which enhanced the grand entrance to the temple of Amun-Ra. Like many other structures and temples at the site, Thutmose's pylon was beautifully adorned with inscriptions and carved reliefs that depicted scenes of his celebrated victories, especially the ones he achieved in the Levant.

However, out of all the expansions he made to the Karnak Temple Complex, the most remarkable was the Sacred Lake. Measuring at least 120 meters by 77 meters, this rectangular lake is considered the largest sacred lake from ancient Egypt. What makes this massive artificial reservoir interesting is the story behind its creation, as it was created as an embodiment of creation itself.

According to Egyptian cosmology, long before the world took its earliest form, before the sky stretched overhead, and before the earth had solidified beneath our feet, there was only Nun. Nun was unlike other important gods of the Egyptian pantheon, like Ra, Osiris, or even Thoth, the god of wisdom. Nun was a being far more ancient. He was infinite and unshaped. Some say he was the eternal flood, while others suggest he was associated with the deep abyss of nothingness and the dark void from which all things would emerge.

It was within this limitless yet silent ocean that the world came to be. From it, a mound of land was born, and it stood alone in the midst of this endless ocean. This sacred mound was known in Egyptian mythology as the benben, and this was where existence began to take shape. Upon it, the first god emerged. This was the self-created ancient god known as Atum. He stood alone on the benben since nothing else existed then.

Later on, from his body, Atum created his children: Shu (the god of air) and Tefnut (the goddess of moisture). From them came Geb (the earth) and Nut (the sky), who, in turn, brought forth the deities known as Osiris, Isis, Set, and Nephthys. These four would be the ones who would shape the destiny of mortals and gods.

As for Nun, he never truly vanished despite the completion of the creation process. Instead, he remained beneath the world. Hidden yet eternal, Nun played a role in nourishing the land just as the Nile's flood brought fortune to the crops every year. This belief inspired the creation of the Sacred Lake; it was meant to be the earthly reflection of the primeval abyss.

The Sacred Lake of Karnak.[51]

The Sacred Lake of Karnak was lined with stone walls and even had stairways that led directly into the water. Surrounding the lake were storerooms and living quarters reserved for the priests. In the morning, before the first rays of Ra emerged from the horizon, the high priests of Amun would go down the stairways into the lake, where they would use the sacred water to purify themselves. This had to be done so that both their bodies and spirits were free from the dust of the mortal world. Only then could the priests enter the temple for other rituals and ceremonial practices. Since the lake was also the home of the sacred geese of Amun (another symbol of creation since the cosmic goose was the one that laid the primordial egg from which creation began), scholars suggest that these priests were also responsible for raising and caring for these creatures. It was important to make sure the geese were in good shape, especially since they would occasionally be used in rituals as living representations of Amun himself.

Interestingly, the lake was said to have never dried up. Besides being used by the priests to purify themselves, the lake was also used in various religious ceremonies and festivals. The waters were used to anoint sacred statues and purify offerings. They were used in ritual processions that celebrated creation, renewal, and divine blessings.

It made sense for later pharaohs who came to the throne after Thutmose III to continue upgrading the lake and its surroundings. The Nubian pharaoh Taharqa, for instance, commissioned the construction of a grand structure on the northern edge of the Sacred Lake. Known by modern scholars as the Edifice of Taharqa, the exact purpose of this structure remains a topic of debate. While some suggest it played a role in religious rituals and royal offerings (especially since Taharqa was known to be extremely devoted to Amun), others claimed it served as temple administration.

Another striking addition near the lake was the sculpture of a scarab (a symbol of the god Khepri) made of granite. It was placed at the northern corner of the lake, a short distance away from the Osirian Temple of Taharqa. This massive scarab, however, was not built on site; it was initially placed in Amenhotep III's mortuary temple, which was located on the west bank of Thebes. Carved entirely in sunk relief, the scarab's pedestal was flattened into the shape of a stela, bearing inscriptions that emphasized the divine renewal of kingship and the eternal cycle of creation. The scarab beetle itself was a sacred emblem of transformation, as the scarab was thought to have rolled the sun across the sky as it emerged from the formless chaos, just as the world had risen from the waters of Nun.

The Osirian Temple of Taharqa.⁸⁸

The Sacred Lake of Karnak was a reminder of the primeval waters of Nun. It was a sacred reservoir where purification was placed above all else. However, like the great temple complex itself, the Sacred Lake was also a portal to something far greater. It was also where the high priests would gather to prepare for one of ancient Egypt's grandest celebrations.

Known as the Festival of Opet, it first gained prominence during the early New Kingdom. This was a time when Egypt had finally gotten free from the Hyksos invaders (they occupied the northern Nile Valley for two centuries). The pharaohs of the rising Eighteenth Dynasty, beginning with Ahmose I, turned Thebes into the political and religious capital of Egypt. The Festival of Opet took place in this city.

Like everything else in Egypt, the timing of the festival was tied to the cycles of the Nile. The festival was celebrated in the second month of Akhet (the season of inundation). During this season, the Egyptians were blessed with the Nile's floodwaters, which deposited rich black silt across the fertile farmlands. As the river replenished the land, Egypt was spiritually renewed through Opet. The Egyptians saw the two as intertwined—the bounty of the flood and the fertility of Amun-Ra (or Amun-Re), the mightiest of the gods. The festival was held to promote the fertility of Amun and the reigning pharaoh, whom the people saw as Amun's spiritual offspring. The pharaoh himself would be symbolically reborn in sacred rituals.

The great avenue that stretched between the Karnak and Luxor temples, lined with rows of sphinxes and ram-headed statues, was the setting for this festival. For miles, the Egyptians would gather, eager to witness the annual divine event. The festival began with high priests moving through the temple corridors. They had to tend to the golden barque of Amun, which was enshrined in his inner sanctum. It was hidden from common eyes at all times, and this was the only time that Amun's presence would leave the great halls of Karnak and journey into the heart of Thebes.

The Luxor Temple, where the barques of Amun, Mut, and Khonsu would arrive during the festival.[88]

When the grand temple doors were thrown open, the people of the kingdom erupted into cheers. Others sang hymns that praised the gods. The priests, who bore the sacred golden barques of Amun, Mut, and Khonsu atop their shoulders, emerged from the temple. They slowly walked, making sure each of their steps was measured. There was no room for mistake since they were carrying the gods themselves. Lotus petals were thrown to the ground as the procession walked past. Clouds of incense rose into the sky, and the rhythmic beating of drums and cymbals could be heard. Dancers, dressed in flowing linen and adorned with exquisite beads, swayed in hypnotic movements; it was as if their bodies mirrored the rhythm of the Nile.

After carrying the divine barques along the Avenue of Sphinxes, the priests gently placed them onto the sacred boats docked at the banks of the Nile. Here, the gods would embark on the most mystical portion of the journey: a symbolic voyage along the Nile. Once in position, the oarsmen would dip their oars into the river, doing so in perfect unison. Onlookers lined the banks, waving palm fronds and offering prayers to the gods.

By the time the divine vessels reached Luxor Temple, the city was already in full celebration. The Egyptians indulged in a feast while musicians entertained them. While laughter and talking echoed through the city streets, the atmosphere inside the temple was different. In the most secluded chambers, the holiest of ceremonies was about to begin.

At the back of Luxor Temple, one could find the "birth room," a dimly lit space tied to the festival. Here, the pharaoh would stand before Amun's divine presence, getting ready for the ritual marriage between the god and the pharaoh. To the ancient Egyptians, it was common knowledge that their pharaoh was the son—or daughter—of Amun. These rulers were thought to be the living embodiment of the divine's will. In this sacred union, the pharaoh ceremonially merged with the god, reborn through a re-crowning ceremony that emphasized his divine legitimacy. This act was not only a spiritual rebirth but also a powerful political statement. The pharaoh's rule was sanctified, and his bond with Amun was reaffirmed, making his divine right to govern Egypt indisputable.

Now that the sacred rites were completed and the pharaoh's rule reaffirmed, it was high time for Amun, Mut, and Khonsu to return to Karnak. The ceremonial boats were readied once more to carry the golden barques of the gods along the Nile. Priests would cast offerings, such as perfumed oils, lotus flowers, and small golden figurines, into the river. These were considered tokens of gratitude for the gods' presence. As the ceremonial boats floated down the Nile, the celebration in the city continued, with the Egyptians dancing and feasting late into the night.

Once the gods arrived through the gates of Karnak once more, they were carried back to the sanctuary. Once the statues of these gods were placed in their sacred chambers, the temple doors were sealed by the priests, signaling the gods' withdrawal into the realm of the heavens. Despite being hidden throughout the year, their presence lingered. The Egyptians knew that the cycle would begin again, just as the Nile would flow and the sun would return each morning.

The festival lasted for a few days. Under Thutmose III, it was celebrated for eleven days, and by the time Ramesses III came to the throne, it had expanded to an astonishing twenty-four days. The Festival of Opet continued well into the New Kingdom and survived even into the Roman period.

Chapter 9 – Cambyses's Lost Army

Egypt was relatively stable when it was ruled by the early pharaohs of the Twenty-sixth Dynasty (also known as the Saite Dynasty). Especially during the reigns of Psamtik I and Necho II, the kingdom witnessed independence from Assyrian dominance. These rulers also successfully rebuilt Egypt's economy and strengthened its military and infrastructure. Necho II launched ambitious projects across the kingdom. He oversaw the construction of the famed Canal of the Pharaohs (also referred to as Necho's Canal), which was the forerunner of the Suez Canal. The pharaoh also launched successful naval expansion campaigns, which further bolstered Egypt's position as a regional power.

In 589 BCE, the mantle was passed to Apries, who inherited the throne from his father, Psamtik II. The pharaoh began his reign with a strong position, yet his later decisions and external circumstances gradually destabilized Egypt. It all began to spiral when Apries had his eyes completely focused on asserting Egyptian power abroad. He supported rebellions against Babylonian control in the Levant and conducted campaigns in Libya. Apries even sent his Egyptian forces to support Libyan allies against Greek settlers but unfortunately suffered a catastrophic defeat.

From here on, Apries's reputation worsened, especially among his army. A mutiny took place among the Egyptian soldiers, as they had been growing discontent with Apries prioritizing foreign mercenaries over them. Apries sent Amasis, a well-respected and high-ranking military officer, to suppress the mutiny. However, the unexpected happened: the Egyptian troops saw Amasis as a capable leader, and they proclaimed him pharaoh instead. A rebellion, now spearheaded by Amasis, was due.

Apries attempted to suppress Amasis and his followers. A civil war broke out, which eventually culminated in a decisive battle in which Amasis and his predominantly native Egyptian forces emerged victorious. Perhaps out of mercy and hoping to avoid future skirmishes by those still loyal to Apries, Amasis treated the captured Apries with some leniency. Herodotus stated that the former pharaoh lived in relative comfort for a time. However, tensions persisted. It was unsure whether Apries simply became a symbol of rebellion for those loyal to him or if he was involved in an attempt to regain power, but the Egyptians were not planning on forgiving him. They pressured Amasis into punishing Apries the way he deserved. Ancient sources claimed that Amasis eventually placed Apries's fate in the hands of the people, who strangled him to death.

Pharaoh Amasis (also known as Ahmose II) went on to rule Egypt for over forty years. He brought the kingdom stability and prosperity. Egyptian pride and cultural identity were restored. The kingdom also maintained its strong ties with the Greeks, and its economic and political strength in the Mediterranean world continued to grow.

However, chaos returned when the Persians saw the rise of Cambyses II, the son of Cyrus the Great. According to Herodotus, Cambyses initially wished to strengthen ties with Egypt. To do this, he requested that Amasis send him a daughter to marry. The pharaoh was unwilling to give his own daughter, yet he did not want to decline the request entirely. So, he sent Nitetis, the daughter of Apries, to the Persian king, claiming that she was one of his own. Unfortunately for Amasis, Nitetis was not planning on staying quiet; she allegedly revealed the deception to Cambyses. The Persian undoubtedly was enraged by this. Apart from this deception, Herodotus also suggested that Amasis's military and diplomatic efforts to resist Persian influence, such as forging alliances with other states (notably Greek city-states like Cyprus and Samos), also contributed to Cambyses's wrath.

The Persian king launched his ambitious campaign to conquer Egypt in 525 BCE, but by this time, Amasis had already died (he passed away only six months prior to the start of the campaign). However, Cambyses was not a person who backed down; the invasion continued to take place, culminating in the decisive Battle of Pelusium in May 525 BCE, where he went against Amasis's son, Pharaoh Psamtik III.

Pelusium was a fortified city on the eastern edge of the Nile Delta. Due to its strategic location, Pelusium was the first line of defense for the Egyptian kingdom. Its fall would give way for the Persians to advance farther into the kingdom. Cambyses, bolstered by years of military experience, commanded a well-disciplined army. His forces were also numerically superior compared to the Egyptian army led by Psamtik III. The young pharaoh knew there was a huge possibility of them losing the battle, so while preparing his troops at Pelusium, Psamtik also ordered the preparation of his capital, Memphis, to withstand a siege.

Initially, the Egyptians at Pelusium were successful in holding their ground. The fortress of Pelusium was well provisioned and strong, and the pharaoh began to see a glimmer of hope. However, Cambyses was cunning. Herodotus wrote that the Persian king had another trick up his sleeve; instead of relying only on military strategies, Cambyses also employed a peculiar psychological tactic, making use of the Egyptians' sacred regard for cats.

According to ancient Egyptian beliefs, cats were closely associated with the goddess Bastet. Bastet was often depicted with the body of a woman and the head of a cat. She was worshiped as the goddess of cats, fertility, and childbirth. The goddess was also believed to possess the power to protect a household from evil spirits and disease. Being a protector deity, Bastet was highly revered, and cats were considered sacred. Herodotus claims that the Egyptians held the animal in such high regard that if a cat were to get caught in a burning building, the Egyptians would prioritize it before their own lives. Harming a cat was seen as a crime, and those who killed one could be sentenced to death.

Cambyses was well aware of this. He ordered his soldiers to paint images of cats on their shields and carry them into battle. Some accounts claimed that the Persians even brought live cats to the battlefield. When the Egyptians saw this, they hesitated. For a moment, they refused to strike for fear of divine retribution. The Persians took this opportunity to wreak havoc on the Egyptian forces. The battlefield quickly turned into a scene of chaos and bloodshed. The Persians made use of their superior tactics and overwhelmed the Egyptian ranks. Psamtik III's vision had come true. His army was indeed unprepared for the scale of Cambyses's assault, and they were crushed.

The defeat was catastrophic for Egypt. The result of this battle also marked the end of the Saite Dynasty. The prosperous kingdom lost its independence. Although Psamtik was able to retreat to Memphis, the tide of war had turned against him.

A painting depicting the Persians using cats to defeat the Egyptians at the Battle of Pelusium.[54]

Whether Herodotus's writings of the Persians using images of cats to tip the scale of war held any truth at all remains a topic of debate. However, we can safely assume that Cambyses's victory at Pelusium was not achieved solely through his military force. The Persians obtained intelligence provided by defectors. One of them was Phanes of Halicarnassus, a Greek mercenary who served as a tactician and advisor under Amasis. Phanes was well versed in Egyptian defenses, and his betrayal was instrumental in the defeat of Egypt.

With Pelusium secured, Cambyses wasted no time in consolidating his control over Egypt. He knew the Egyptians placed religion and culture above all else. Therefore, one of his first acts was to seek the favor of the goddess Neith, the primordial goddess often associated with creation, wisdom, and warfare. As one of Egypt's most ancient and highly revered deities, her temple in Sais was a focal point of Egyptian spirituality and governance. Cambyses hoped that by paying homage to the goddess, he could portray himself as the rightful ruler of the kingdom who respected its traditions instead of a foreign conqueror.

Then, the Persian king turned his attention to Memphis, the key city to controlling both Upper and Lower Egypt. Just as Psamtik had expected, Cambyses laid siege to it. Their engineering and tactical prowess were remarkable because, despite having time to prepare, the defenders found their hope of success chipped away as the seconds went by. Eventually, Memphis fell, marking a decisive moment in the Persian conquest of Egypt. Psamtik III, who had sought refuge in the city following his defeat at Pelusium, was taken prisoner. He planned a rebellion to overthrow the Persians but achieved no success.

As a result, Psamtik was forced to drink bull's blood. In ancient times, it was believed that drinking bull's blood was lethal or could even drive a person mad. This version of Psamtik's death was narrated in the *Histories* by Herodotus, so this might be more legend than fact. Since bull's blood contains high levels of iron and protein, drinking it in large quantities may result in iron poisoning or hemochromatosis. Other sources suggest that the blood was possibly poisoned to hasten the process. Poisoned or not (and if the story is true), Psamtik likely experienced a daunting episode of nausea and vomiting before going through organ failure, leading to his death.

With Memphis now firmly in his grasp, Cambyses adopted the title of pharaoh and began aligning himself with Egyptian religious practices and traditions. Herodotus claimed that his rule was ruthless, with cities and temples across the kingdom often facing lootings and desecrations. Yet, his records need to be taken with a grain of salt, especially since no contemporary Egyptian sources ever recorded the looting of temples.

From Memphis, Cambyses made his way to the spiritual heart of Upper Egypt: Thebes. This city was known for its temples dedicated to the mighty deity Amun. Here, Cambyses made his desire to be named the legitimate pharaoh of Egypt known. He sought acknowledgment from the priests of the oracle of Amun at the Siwa Oasis. The oracle's recognition would affirm Cambyses's right to rule in the eyes of his new subjects. Being acknowledged by the oracle of Amun would imply that Cambyses had the gods' blessing. This would reinforce his authority, not only in Egypt but also in the broader ancient world, where such divine endorsements carried significant weight.

However, the priests refused to acknowledge him as the kingdom's rightful ruler. Their rejection enraged the Persian king. Cambyses saw their defiance as a direct affront to his authority.

This did not deter the king's ambitions to expand his empire. To further assert dominance over the region, Cambyses launched another bold invasion campaign, this time into Ethiopia. He launched this campaign from Thebes. Yet, the Persian king did not forget about the defiant priests at Siwa. He divided his forces. While he led half of his troops southward into Ethiopian territory, Cambyses also detached a contingent of fifty thousand men toward the Siwa Oasis so that they could punish those who refused to acknowledge him as the rightful ruler.

The journey to Siwa was challenging. Under the scorching desert sun, the troops had to cross treacherous terrain as they navigated the desolate expanses of the Egyptian desert. Modern scholars suggest that the El-Kharga Oasis was their first major stop. Here, the troops must have rested and replenished their water supplies before continuing their grueling march. Their next stop remains a mystery; El-Kharga was the last place that the contingent was last seen.

A relief depicting Persian soldiers during the time of Cambyses.[85]

If we were to take account of Herodotus's writings, the historian claimed that all fifty thousand men faced their demise at the hands of Mother Nature. As they continued their journey, Cambyses's men were eventually met with vast columns of whirling sand driven by powerful desert winds. This brutal sandstorm engulfed each of the soldiers and buried him deep beneath the dunes. As the sandstorm calmed down, it erased all traces of their presence, leaving both historians and archaeologists with only questions about the disappearance of the army.

Theories and Speculations Surrounding the Disappearance of Cambyses's Men

The exact route taken by Cambyses's lost army has long been a subject of debate among historians. Many agree that the soldiers marched southwest from Thebes, traversing through one of the harshest landscapes on Earth toward the Siwa Oasis. Alexander the Great once embarked on a pilgrimage to Siwa. However, this took place two centuries later, and the distance of his chosen route was likely shorter compared to the one taken by Cambyses's men. But despite being shorter in distance, Alexander and his men also went through multiple obstacles. Ancient accounts even suggested that they would not have succeeded if it were not for divine intervention. If the great conqueror faced difficulties traversing the terrain some two centuries later, it is not surprising that Cambyses's men had problems too. Their chosen route, which plunged them directly into the heart of the desert, undoubtedly exposed the troops to unrelenting heat, scarce water supplies, and disorientation.

Of course, logistical challenges might have also played a role in the fate of the lost army. The desert was unforgiving with its searing daytime temperatures and freezing nights. These two brutal differences would have sapped the strength of even the strongest soldiers. Herodotus suggested that the army ran out of provisions rather quickly. As a result, they were left with no choice but to rely on what little they could scavenge. The Greek historian wrote that the army soon grew beyond desperate to the point they ate grass. When no grass could be seen, some of them resorted to cannibalism. Herodotus's accounts are often filled with exaggeration and bias, yet these grim details show the dire conditions faced by the soldiers.

Another theory talks about the army using an incorrect map, which led them to march either in circles or in the direction of an uninhabitable region of the desert. Coupled with the lack of significant landmarks, it made sense that the soldiers wandered aimlessly for an extended period of time. It could also be plausible that because of logistical mismanagement, combined with the natural hazards of the desert, the troops lost their supply wagons. Without enough supplies and equipment, Cambyses's men were left vulnerable in the brutal environment.

Obliterated by an Ambush

While the theory of the army consumed by a relentless sandstorm is considered the most popular to this date, there is another theory that involves an ambush. This particular theory centers around a figure known as Petubastis III. Operating from the remote Dakhla Oasis, Petubastis probably heard the news of Cambyses's men nearing his territory. Leveraging on the isolated location of the oasis and its natural defenses, along with the Persians' lack of knowledge about the region, Petubastis thought he was given a golden opportunity to finally challenge Persian authority. After all, Petubastis was considered a champion of Egyptian independence, and he had the support of local militias who deeply resented Persian control.

The desert had clearly allied with Petubastis and his forces; the vast and arid expanse had already weakened the Persian forces, which were most likely already struggling with logistical challenges. Dehydration, disorientation, and exhaustion might have terrorized the soldiers, leaving them vulnerable despite their superior skills obtained from years of war. Therefore, it would not have been impossible for Petubastis and his forces to gain the upper hand. When they launched an ambush near the Dakhla Oasis, the Egyptians made use of their effective guerilla tactics. The desert was turned into a trap, and the disoriented Persians were almost immediately overwhelmed.

This success benefited Petubastis greatly. This victory opened the gates for Petubastis to declare himself pharaoh in Memphis. However, when Darius I rose to the throne to succeed Cambyses, the new king was said to have worked to suppress this narrative. To avoid telling the world of the Persians' defeat, Darius crafted a tale of a sandstorm that swallowed the army whole.

The Biggest Discovery

Some might agree that the Sahara Desert has long been a graveyard of mysteries. Its vast and continuously shifting sands are capable of swallowing the histories of different civilizations, with Cambyses's lost army being among them. However, in 1996, the mystery began to crack as more archaeological evidence was uncovered. Spearheaded by twin Italian archaeologists named Angelo and Alfredo Castiglioni, the expedition was initially launched to investigate the presence of iron meteorites near the Bahariya Oasis (a small oasis close to Siwa). What they found, however, shed light on one of history's most mysterious disappearances.

As the archaeologists toiled under the relentless sun, they suddenly noticed a strange artifact buried deep beneath the sand. To untrained eyes, this object was nothing but a simple half-buried pot. However, even with a single glance, the brothers knew it was a fragment of a long-forgotten past. Upon further excavation, they soon unearthed more evidence, all of which pointed to that location as a site where an important event occurred. First, they discovered bleached bones and fragments of what might have once been an army. Then, the team of archaeologists uncovered a natural rock formation. Measuring about 114 feet long, close to 6 feet high, and 10 feet deep, its size and shape appeared almost too perfect; it was almost as if it had been used as a refuge for those caught in a sandstorm.

Also beneath this rock formation, the archaeologists found relics of ancient warfare, including a bronze dagger and arrow tips. Less than a mile from the natural shelter were remnants of more treasures, including a silver bracelet, an earring, and spherical trinkets that most likely belonged to a necklace. Interestingly, scientific testing revealed that all of these objects—both the ancient weapons and jewelry—dated to the Achaemenid period, placing them squarely within Cambyses's era.

These findings raised eyebrows. For centuries, scholars and historians held the belief that the army marched along the caravan paths through the Dakhla and Farafra Oases, though no concrete evidence has emerged to fully support this speculation. However, with the findings of the Castiglioni brothers, historians are able to open the door to a whole different theory. It is likely that the army had taken a different southern route. Beginning from El Kargha, they presumably ventured westward to Gilf Kebir. Then, the brothers headed north through Wadi Abd el

Melik toward Siwa. The reasons behind the army's decision to use this path instead of the traditional caravan route were probably simple. They could bypass Egyptian-controlled oases, thus minimizing the possibility of them facing resistance or ambush. This way, they could make their way to Siwa undisturbed.

Of course, each theory needs to be supported by concrete evidence, and the Castiglioni brothers were eager to conduct geological surveys along this alternative route. The brothers discovered desiccated water sources and artificial wells constructed from hundreds of water pots buried deep beneath the soft sand. This discovery answered one of the questions surrounding this theory: how did the army sustain themselves while they traversed this longer and harsher terrain? Furthermore, thermoluminescence dating confirmed the pottery's age; they all aligned with Cambyses's time.

The investigations culminated in the year 2002, with the brothers going back to the site of their initial discoveries. They proposed that it could be plausible that the army had used ancient maps that mistakenly placed the temple of Amun in this specific area. The soldiers, thinking that they had arrived at their destination, were then caught off guard, not by mortal enemies but by Mother Nature. The khamsin (a hot, fierce, and unpredictable southeasterly wind) was heading toward them, sweeping everything across the Sahara. Panic undoubtedly terrorized the soldiers. Some might have sought refuge under a natural shelter (like the one discovered by the Castiglioni brothers in the 1990s), while those who managed to escape possibly made their way to Sitra Lake.

Why there were no traces of the survivors remains a mystery. It is possible that since they had failed their mission to reach Siwa, they decided to go incognito, fearing the wrath of their king. After all, ancient armies were often held to strict standards. Failure, especially on such an important—or rather vengeful—mission, could easily result in severe punishment. Apart from this, the lack of evidence could also be a result of the harsh environment of the Sahara. The intense heat and erosion would have made it difficult for any physical remains or artifacts to survive the test of time. It is also worth noting that it was common for historical records to be intentionally altered or omitted to erase any sort of failures.

The brothers heard stories by the Bedouin where they claimed to have seen white bones emerging from the sand during certain wind conditions. Upon further investigations, a mass grave was discovered near the excavation site of the natural shelter, which contained hundreds of skeletons and skulls bleached by centuries of exposure to the harsh desert sun and winds. Persian arrowheads and a horse bit were also unearthed, all of which were identical to depictions in ancient Persian reliefs. A sword was reportedly discovered as well, but unfortunately, it had already been sold to American tourists. With all these findings, it seemed likely that the final resting place of Cambyses's famed lost army had been discovered, buried beneath over sixteen feet of sand.

Nevertheless, the mystery never got its official ending. The Castiglioni brothers reported their findings and handed over the artifacts to the Geological Survey of Egypt. However, they never heard back. Even so, the brothers were certain that they had successfully come closer than anyone to solving the disappearance.

Conclusion

Some describe ancient Egypt as a treasure trove of mysteries, while others picture it as an endless labyrinth of forgotten stories, hidden tombs, and unanswered questions. It is indeed one of the most intriguing civilizations. For many centuries, it has fascinated not only historians, scholars, and archaeologists but also avid history enthusiasts, curious readers, and mystery lovers. With its grand structures, cryptic texts, supposed curses, and secrets, this civilization attracts the attention of even those who have very little interest in history.

Despite many traces of the civilization having been unearthed, from the remnants of the pyramids and temples to the houses of the artisans and papyrus full of spells and hymns, there is still so much that remains buried deep beneath the sands. One can only wonder what else lies in the tombs that have yet to be discovered. What other secrets do the ancient hieroglyphs hold? Which cities are still under the desert, doing nothing but remaining silent until they are discovered once more? Every discovery gives us new questions to ponder and brings forth another piece of the puzzle.

It is safe to say that Egypt remains an unfinished story. There are still missing chapters waiting to see the light once more. But perhaps this is why Egypt continues to capture the imagination of so many. With every excavation, every deciphered text, and every newly uncovered relic, new details emerge, new mysteries unfold, and new perspectives reshape what we think we know.

Here's another book by Matt Clayton that you might like

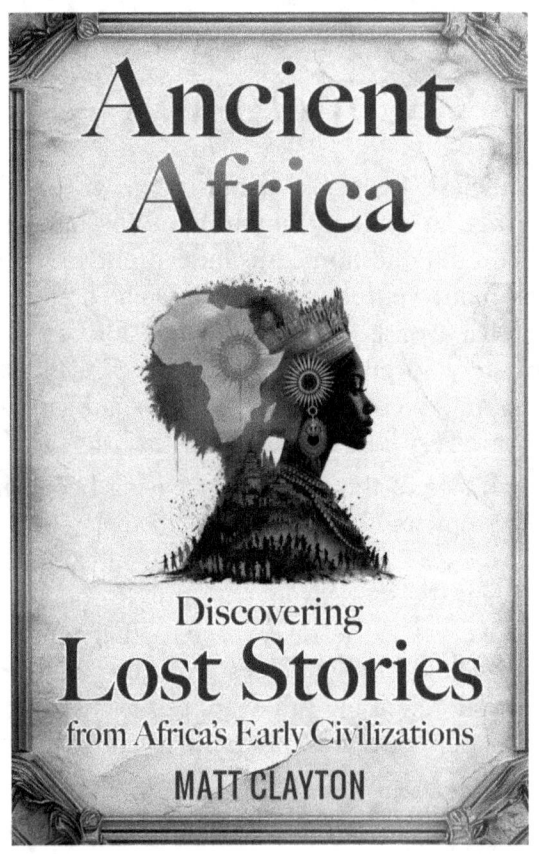

Free Bonus from Captivating History (Available for a Limited time)

Hi History Lovers!

Now you have a chance to join our exclusive history list so you can get your first history ebook for free as well as discounts and a potential to get more history books for free!

Simply visit the link below to join.

Or, Scan the QR code!

captivatinghistory.com/ebook

Also, make sure to follow us on Facebook, X, and YouTube by searching for Captivating History.

Bibliography

Bárta, Miroslav. "The Search for Imhotep: Tomb of Architect-Turned-God Remains a Mystery." *ARCE*, Accessed January 1. arce.org/resource/search-imhotep-tomb-architect-turned-god-remains-mystery.

Barton, Marc. "Imhotep – the First Physician - Past Medical History." *Past Medical History*, April 28, 2018. www.pastmedicalhistory.co.uk/imhotep-the-first-physician.

Cummins, Elizabeth. "Tutankhamun's Tomb (Innermost Coffin and Death Mask)." *Smart History.* Accessed January 28, 2025. smarthistory.org/tutankhamuns-tomb-innermost-coffin-and-death-mask.

De Lazaro, Enrico. "Mystery Surrounding Lost Army of Persian King Cambyses II May Have Been Solved." *Sci.News*, June 19, 2014. www.sci.news/archaeology/science-lost-army-persian-king-cambyses-ii-02002.html.

Escolano-Poveda, Marina. "Imhotep: A Sage Between Fiction and Reality." *ARCE*, Accessed January 10, 2025. arce.org/resource/imhotep-sage-between-fiction-and-reality.

Gillan, Joanna. "The Lost Labyrinth of Ancient Egypt – Part 1." *Ancient Origins.* January 13, 2020. https://www.ancient-origins.net/ancient-places-africa/lost-labyrinth-ancient-egypt-part-1-002033

HistoricalEve. "Ramses III Against the Sea Peoples." *The Archaeologist*, October 27, 2022. www.thearchaeologist.org/blog/ramses-iii-against-the-sea-peoples?utm_source=chatgpt.com#google_vignette.

Holloway, April. "The Lost Labyrinth of Ancient Egypt – Part 2." *Ancient Origins.* September 3, 2014. https://www.ancient-origins.net/ancient-places-africa/lost-labyrinth-ancient-egypt-part-2-002034

Holloway, April. "The Lost Labyrinth of Ancient Egypt – Part 3: Uncovering Its Location." *Ancient Origins.* September 4, 2014. https://www.ancient-origins.net/ancient-places-africa/lost-labyrinth-ancient-egypt-part-3-uncovering-its-location-002039

Litecky, Tessa. "The Opet Festival: Rejuvenation of the Gods." *Mused.* Accessed February 3, 2025. mused.com/stories/127/the-opet-festival-rejuvenation-of-the-gods.

Lorenzi, Rossella. "Vanished Persian Army Said Found in Desert." *NBC News,* Nov 10, 2009. www.nbcnews.com/id/wbna33791672.

Mana, Davide. "The Lost Army of Cambyses." *Karavansara,* Sept 30, 2021. karavansara.live/2021/09/30/the-lost-army-of-cambyses.

Margaret. "'Seeking Senenmut: Statues, Status and Scandal' Campbell Price (EEG Meeting Talk)." *Other People's Tales,* June 15, 2016. writeups.talesfromthetwolands.org/2016/06/15/seeking-senenmut-statues-status-and-scandal-campbell-price-eeg-meeting-talk.

Mark, Joshua J., and RÃ©Mih. "Deir el-Medina." *World History Encyclopedia,* Feb. 2025, www.worldhistory.org/Deir_el-Medina.

Mark, Joshua J. "Imhotep." *World History Encyclopedia,* Feb 16, 2016. www.worldhistory.org/imhotep.

Mark, Joshua J. "Sea Peoples." *World History Encyclopedia,* September 2, 2009. https://www.worldhistory.org/Sea_Peoples/.

Mark, Joshua J. "The Battle of Pelusium: A Victory Decided by Cats." *World History Encyclopedia,* July 10,. 2017. www.worldhistory.org/article/43/the-battle-of-pelusium-a-victory-decided-by-cats.

Mark, Joshua J. "Third Intermediate Period of Egypt." *World History Encyclopedia,* October 11, 2016. www.worldhistory.org/Third_Intermediate_Period_of_Egypt.

Maydana, Sebastián. "Devouring Gods! What Was the Ancient Egyptian Cannibal Hymn?" *TheCollector,* September 20, 2022. www.thecollector.com/ancient-egyptian-cannibal-hymn.

Penner, Jay. *"The Story of the Lost Army of Cambyses." Jay Penner.* Accessed February 2, 2025. jaypenner.com/blog/the-story-of-the-lost-army-of-cambyses.

Ryan, Donald P. "24 Hours in Ancient Egypt: A Day in the Life of the People Who Lived There." Michael O'Mara Books.

Samir, Samar. "Famine Stela: A Piece of Pharaonic Diary." *EgyptToday,* July 15, 2018. www.egypttoday.com/Article/4/54056/Famine-Stela-A-piece-of-Pharaonic-diary.

"Imhotep Vizier of Works." *The Curious Egyptologist,* July 4, 2022. thecuriousegyptologist.com/2022/07/04/imhotep-vizier-of-works.

"Pyramid of Unas." *Lonely Planet.* Accessed January 25, 2025.
www.lonelyplanet.com/egypt/saqqara-memphis-dahshur/attractions/pyramid-of-unas/a/poi-sig/1501661/1330429.

"Tantamani: The Last Pharaoh of the 25th Dynasty of Egypt." *World History Edu,* November 5, 2024. worldhistoryedu.com/tantamani-the-last-pharaoh-of-the-25th-dynasty-of-egypt.

"The Cannibalism Hymn of Pharaoh Unas: Ancient Egypt's Most Disturbing Inscription." *History Skills,* Accessed January 14, 2025.
www.historyskills.com/classroom/ancient-history/cannibalism-hymn-of-unas/?srsltid=AfmBOopDtQadOkSUkm0H_sTltw9Mw-YqD5kPeLd7d1M-vwQXHzcRUiuo.

"The Lost Labyrinth of Ancient Egypt." *Historical Eve.* June 22, 2021.
https://historicaleve.com/lost-labyrinth-of-ancient-egypt/

"The Sacred Lake in Karnak Temple Luxor | History, Facts, Pharaonic Temples." *Goota Travel,* September 3, 2022. gootatravel.com/ancient-egypt-civilization/pharaonic-temples/the-sacred-lake-in-karnak-temple-luxor.

"The Sea Peoples: Who Were They, and How Much Chaos Did They Create in the Bronze Age?" *World History Edu,* October 10, 2024.
worldhistoryedu.com/the-sea-peoples/

Image Sources

1 The Wellcome Collection, CC BY 4.0
<https://creativecommons.org/licenses/by/4.0>, via Wikimedia Commons:
https://commons.wikimedia.org/wiki/File:An_invocation_to_I-em-
hetep,_the_Egyptian_deity_of_medicine._Wellcome_V0018149.jpg

2 Mastaba.jpg: Unknown. Originally uploaded by Oesermaatra0069 at 2006-03-
12.derivative work: Master Uegly, CC BY-SA 3.0
<http://creativecommons.org/licenses/by-sa/3.0/>, via Wikimedia Commons:
https://commons.wikimedia.org/wiki/File:Mastaba_schematics.svg

3 Francisco Anzola, CC BY 2.0 <https://creativecommons.org/licenses/by/2.0>, via
Wikimedia Commons: https://commons.wikimedia.org/wiki/File:Zoser
Pyramid(2347235367).jpg

4 Morburre, CC BY-SA 3.0 <https://creativecommons.org/licenses/by-sa/3.0>, via
Wikimedia Commons: https://commons.wikimedia.org/wiki/File:Sehel-
steleFamine.jpg

5 Metropolitan Museum of Art, CC0, via Wikimedia Commons:
https://commons.wikimedia.org/wiki/File:Imhotep,_donated_by_Padisu_MET_DP
164134.jpg

6 https://commons.wikimedia.org/wiki/File:Edwin_Smith_Papyrus_v2.jpg

7 Aidan McRae Thomson, CC BY-SA 2.0 <https://creativecommons.org/licenses/by-
sa/2.0>, via Wikimedia Commons: https://commons.wikimedia.org/wiki
/File:Pyramid_Texts_in_Unas%E2%80%99_Pyramid_2017.jpg

8 Olaf Tausch, CC BY 3.0 <https://creativecommons.org/licenses/by/3.0>, via
Wikimedia Commons: https://commons.wikimedia.org/wiki/File:Unas-
Pyramide_(Sakkara)_13.jpg

9 https://commons.wikimedia.org/wiki/File:01_unas_causeway.jpg

10 Rama, CC BY-SA 3.0 FR <https://creativecommons.org/licenses/by-sa/3.0/fr/deed.en>, via Wikimedia Commons: https://commons.wikimedia.org/wiki/File:Bedouins_starving_in_the_desert-E_17381-IMG_9845-gradient.jpg

11 ArdadN, Jeff Dahl, CC BY-SA 3.0 <https://creativecommons.org/licenses/by-sa/3.0>, via Wikimedia Commons: https://commons.wikimedia.org/wiki/File:Egypt_NK_edit.svg

12 https://commons.wikimedia.org/wiki/File:Medinet_Habu_Ramses _III._Tempel_Nordostwand_Abzeichnung_01.jpg

13 Andrew®, CC BY 2.0 <https://creativecommons.org/licenses/by/2.0>, via Wikimedia Commons: https://commons.wikimedia.org/wiki/File:Deir_el-Medina_ruins_(2009a).jpg

14 Fotograf/Photographer: Peter J. Bubenik (1995), CC BY-SA 2.0 <https://creativecommons.org/licenses/by-sa/2.0>, via Wikimedia Commons: https://commons.wikimedia.org/wiki/File:Luxor,_Tal_der_K%C3%B6nige_(1995,_ 860x605).jpg

15 EditorfromMars, CC BY-SA 4.0 <https://creativecommons.org/licenses/by-sa/4.0>, via Wikimedia Commons: https://commons.wikimedia.org/wiki/File: Inside_Pharaoh_Tutankhamun%27s_tomb,_18th_dynasty.jpg

16 Ad Meskens, CC BY-SA 3.0 <https://creativecommons.org/licenses/by-sa/3.0>, via Wikimedia Commons: https://commons.wikimedia.org/wiki/File: Mortuary_Temple_of_Hatshepsut_01.jpg

17 Osama Shukir Muhammed Amin FRCP(Glasg), CC BY-SA 4.0 <https://creativecommons.org/licenses/by-sa/4.0>, via Wikimedia Commons: https://commons.wikimedia.org/wiki/File:Stone_inscribed_with_the_name_of_Sene nmut,_from_Thebes,_Egypt._Neues_Museum,_Berlin.jpg

18 British Museum, CC BY-SA 3.0 <http://creativecommons.org/licenses/by-sa/3.0/>, via Wikimedia Commons: https://commons.wikimedia.org/wiki/File: BlockStatueOfSenenmutAndNeferura-LeftProfile-BritishMuseum-August19-08.jpg

19 Metropolitan Museum of Art, CC0, via Wikimedia Commons: https://commons.wikimedia.org/wiki/File:Seated_Statue_of_Hatshepsut_MET_Hat shepsut2012.jpg

20 Kimberlym21, CC BY-SA 4.0 <https://creativecommons.org/licenses/by-sa/4.0>, via Wikimedia Commons: https://commons.wikimedia.org/wiki/File: Mortuary_Temple_of_Hatshepsut,_Egypt.jpg

21 Edal Anton Lefterov, CC BY-SA 3.0 <https://creativecommons.org/licenses/by-sa/3.0>, via Wikimedia Commons: https://commons.wikimedia.org/wiki/File:Tomb-of-Senenmut.jpg

22 Keith Schengili-Roberts, CC BY-SA 3.0 <http://creativecommons.org/licenses/by-sa/3.0/>, via Wikimedia Commons:

https://commons.wikimedia.org/wiki/File:Senenmut-BrownQuartziteSarcophagus_MetropolitanMuseum.png

23 Toni Pecoraro, CC BY-SA 4.0 <https://creativecommons.org/licenses/by-sa/4.0>, via Wikimedia Commons: https://commons.wikimedia.org/wiki/File:Egyptian_labyrinth.jpg

24 https://commons.wikimedia.org/wiki/File:%D0%9B%D0%B0%D0%B1%D1%96%D1%80%D0%B8%D0%BD%D1%82_%D0%B2_%D0%A5%D0%B0%D0%B2%D0%B0%D1%80%D1%96,_%D0%BE%D0%BF%D0%B8%D1%81%D0%B0%D0%BD%D0%B8%D0%B9_%D0%93%D0%B5%D1%80%D0%BE%D0%B4%D0%BE%D1%82%D0%BE%D0%BC.jpg

25 LassiHU, CC BY-SA 4.0 <https://creativecommons.org/licenses/by-sa/4.0>, via Wikimedia Commons: https://commons.wikimedia.org/wiki/File:Gebel_Barkal.jpg

26 Bertramz, CC BY 3.0 <https://creativecommons.org/licenses/by/3.0>, via Wikimedia Commons: https://commons.wikimedia.org/wiki/File:Al-Kurru,main_pyramid.jpg

27 Cornell University Library, CC BY 2.0 <https://creativecommons.org/licenses/by/2.0>, via Wikimedia Commons: https://commons.wikimedia.org/wiki/File:Temple_Complex_at_Karnak.jpg

28 René Hourdry, CC BY-SA 4.0 <https://creativecommons.org/licenses/by-sa/4.0>, via Wikimedia Commons: https://commons.wikimedia.org/wiki/File:Temple_de_Louxor_53.jpg

29 Sara Nabih, CC BY-SA 4.0 <https://creativecommons.org/licenses/by-sa/4.0>, via Wikimedia Commons: https://commons.wikimedia.org/wiki/File:Karnak_Temple,_Ram_Road.JPG

30 Dennis G. Jarvis, CC BY-SA 2.0 <https://creativecommons.org/licenses/by-sa/2.0>, via Wikimedia Commons: https://commons.wikimedia.org/wiki/File:Egypt-3B-009_-_Festival_Hall_of_Tuthmosis_III_(2216561709).jpg

31 Warren LeMay from Chicago, IL, United States, CC0, via Wikimedia Commons: https://commons.wikimedia.org/wiki/File:Sacred_Lake,_Karnak_Temple,_Luxor,_LG,_EGY_(48009488536).jpg

32 Warren LeMay from Chicago, IL, United States, CC0, via Wikimedia Commons: https://commons.wikimedia.org/wiki/File:Osrian_Temple_of_Taharqa,_Karnak_Temple,_Luxor,_LG,_EGY_(48009600862).jpg

33 https://commons.wikimedia.org/wiki/File:Luxor_temple_2.JPG

34 https://commons.wikimedia.org/wiki/File:Le_roi_Cambyse_au_si%C3%A8ge_de_P%C3%A9luse_par_Paul-Marie_Lenoir.jpg

35 Pergamon Museum, CC BY 2.0 <https://creativecommons.org/licenses/by/2.0>, via Wikimedia Commons: https://commons.wikimedia.org/wiki/File:Persian_warriors_from_Berlin_Museum.jpg

www.ingramcontent.com/pod-product-compliance
Lightning Source LLC
Chambersburg PA
CBHW071205120626
46546CB00006B/2421